Dinefwr ~~Castle~~
Dryslwyn Castle

Sian E. Rees BA, PhD, FSA
and Chris Caple BSc, PhD, ACR, FIIC, FSA

A History of the Castles

Introduction

For the year 1093, the native Welsh annals record that Rhys ap Tewdwr, prince of Deheubarth, was slain in battle with the Normans — the 'Frenchmen who were inhabiting Brycheiniog'. As the scribe of *Brut y Tywysogyon* (*Chronicle of the Princes*) went on to lament, 'then fell the kingdom of the Britons'. He barely exaggerated, for the advance of the invaders into south-west Wales in the years which followed was rapid and devastating. So much so that by the early twelfth century the three provinces of the ancient kingship of Deheubarth — as well as those of Brycheiniog, Gwent and Morgannwg — formed part of the March of Wales, held largely under firm and almost continuous Norman control. For the Deheubarth dynasty of princes in the south-west, the onslaught and its aftermath proved crushing. Yet less than a hundred years later, native authority in the kingdom had been almost entirely reconstituted under Rhys's grandson, the great Rhys ap Gruffudd (d. 1197). And, as we shall see, the histories of the Welsh castles at Dinefwr (the main seat of the kingdom) and Dryslwyn were only just beginning.

Both sites now stand among the most treasured monuments of the Middle Ages to be found anywhere in Wales; they continue to occupy a place of great affection in the minds and traditions of the Welsh people. What survives in terms of upstanding remains dates largely from the thirteenth century, and was the work of Rhys ap Gruffudd's heirs and successors. It seems likely, for example, that the great round towers or keeps — that which dominates the centre of Dinefwr and another of very similar design at Dryslwyn — were thrown up in a period of relative stability under his son, Rhys Gryg (d. 1233), or a little later. Further building along the rocky and naturally protected sites meant that, by the time of the Welsh wars of King Edward I (1272–1307) in 1276–77 and 1282–83, both castles had become formidable defensive obstacles.

From the late thirteenth through to the fifteenth century, when the castles served as centres of royal authority and administration, repairs and new building occasionally featured to a greater or lesser extent. By the end of the Middle Ages, however, the sites had fallen into decline and they were gradually to become ivy-clad ruins. Subsequently, Dinefwr in particular was to see a new lease of life in the late seventeenth and eighteenth centuries. With the top of its keep converted to a summerhouse, it was to become a Romantic element in a landscape of great Picturesque beauty.

Modern investigation of the architecture and archaeology of the castles began in the 1980s. The walls of Dryslwyn were excavated from beneath centuries of collapsed debris, and those of Dinefwr were gradually cleared of their verdant but harmful shroud. Following extensive conservation work, the sites have been laid out for public display and are now maintained by Cadw, the historic environment service of the Welsh Assembly Government.

At Dinefwr, Cadw works closely with the Wildlife Trust of South and West Wales — which owns the castle and placed it in State care — and also with the National Trust, which owns Newton House and the surrounding landscaped park.

Early History

Even at first glimpse, it is clear that the long ridge occupied by Dinefwr and the rocky knoll on which Dryslwyn is perched are positions of the most extraordinary defensive strength. Suggestions that prehistoric fortifications may underlie the medieval castles are plausible. Topographically, the sites are highly suitable for earlier defensive settlements, but,

Dinefwr Castle still towers above the river Tywi. Although its origins are obscure, the castle's close association with Rhys ap Gruffudd (d. 1197) has ensured it a place of great affection in the minds of the Welsh people.

Opposite: Dryslwyn Castle stands prominently atop a small and steep-sided hill at the centre of the broad Tywi valley. Like neighbouring Dinefwr, it was an important stronghold raised by medieval Welsh princes who ruled over the ancient kingship of Deheubarth.

The Book of St Teilo, *now more commonly known as the* Gospels of St Chad *or the* Lichfield Gospels, *was in the possession of the important religious community at Llandeilo Fawr, not far from Dinefwr, during the ninth and tenth centuries. Marginal notes, as shown on this page, are not only the earliest evidence of written Welsh but also testify to the significance of Llandeilo Fawr (Dean and Chapter of Lichfield Cathedral Ms. 1).*

to date, no evidence has been found to support this notion. However, the discovery and partial excavation of two superimposed Roman forts within Dinefwr Park (p. 33) supplements earlier reports of mosaics and coins being uncovered there. Moreover, references in the *Book of St Teilo* and the *Book of Llandaff* indicate that nearby Llandeilo Fawr was a place of great significance well before the arrival of the Normans. In particular, the church of Llandeilo Fawr is traditionally associated with Teilo, the sixth-century early Christian saint, and it may well have been the site of his *clas*, or mother church, as well as his burial place. Two carved stone cross-heads, still to be seen in the medieval parish church, are a clear sign that a religious community survived here through to the ninth or early tenth century.

The Welsh lawbooks of the medieval period, the earliest of which is a text of the thirteenth century, accord to Dinefwr a special status as the principal court of the kingdom of Deheubarth. Indeed, the lawbooks, which emanate from the kingdom of Deheubarth itself, accord Dinefwr parity with Aberffraw, the chief court of the kingdom of Gwynedd. Gold was payable to the kings who ruled from these courts whenever they were offended, whereas cattle were paid to other kings. The phraseology of the lawyers' statements may give Dinefwr an aura of antiquity, but written sources do not suggest that the castle has any history earlier than the twelfth century. It is thus impossible to establish whether the site had any links with early

kings of the dynasty of Deheubarth, such as Hywel Dda (d. 949–50), or Rhys ap Tewdwr (d. 1093). Certainly, the earliest reference to the castle of Dinefwr in historical sources belongs to the period of Rhys ap Gruffudd, the Lord Rhys.

Despite the uncertainty, we can be sure that by the end of the twelfth century Dinefwr had come to occupy a place of great significance in the annals of Welsh history. In the 1190s, Gerald of Wales (d. 1223) described it as one of the three ancient Welsh royal seats, along with Aberffraw in Gwynedd and Pengwern in Powys. It was, he wrote, the place where the 'palace of south Wales used to be ... well protected by its site and surrounded by woods'. Just a few decades later, in a letter to King Henry III (1216–72), Prince Llywelyn the Great (d. 1240) referred to the 'once famous now ruined' castle at Dinefwr, to which 'as the capital of Deheubarth', he went on, 'pertained the dignities of the whole of that province'.

Lack of excavation means that, for the moment, such intimations regarding Dinefwr's antiquity must remain unproven. Indeed, it seems likely that Dinefwr's importance would have been exaggerated for political reasons by the successors of the Lord Rhys. Added to this, we may note the silence of the chronicles and other written sources regarding the existence of a castle before Rhys's time — a curious omission if so important a stronghold had been built there. Present evidence suggests very strongly that the history of the castle began during the rule of the Lord Rhys.

In his letter to Henry III (1216–72), written in September 1220, Llywelyn the Great (d. 1240) described Dinefwr as 'once famous now ruined', a castle to which previously 'pertained the dignities' of the whole of Deheubarth. Despite the ambiguous evidence for Dinefwr's antiquity, it is clear that from early on the castle was manipulated as a potent symbol of independent Welsh rule (The National Archives: PRO, SC 1/4/18).

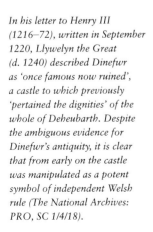

The Lord Rhys

Brut y Tywysogyon records that in 1165 Rhys ap Gruffudd 'took Cantref Mawr and the castle of Dinefwr', holding them for his own until his death in 1197. As the name of Dinefwr conjures up the might of the capital seat of the kingship of Deheubarth, that of the Lord Rhys personifies its figurehead. One of the greatest Welsh leaders of the twelfth century, he was able to withstand the power of the Anglo-Norman lords of the March, supported on occasion by the intervention of King Henry II (1154–89) of England, and recreate the kingdom. He was then able to take advantage of the king's more conciliatory policy in the period after 1171 to maintain a stable authority for many years. Deheubarth flourished over a period of relative peace and general harmony, with Welsh culture and religious life, as well as legal and administrative affairs, all benefiting from Rhys's patronage and self-assured governance.

Above all, Rhys was a supreme realist. He was not tempted to overreach himself by taking on the might of the Anglo-Norman lords of the southern March; nor did he try to extend authority over the native rulers of Gwynedd and Powys. Not that he was averse to military action. In the early years of his life, Rhys was forced to resort to strenuous military effort to restore the authority of his lineage over a kingdom torn apart by Anglo-Norman aggression. Gradually, over a period of more than twenty years, he re-established a single power over the lands of Ystrad Tywi, Ceredigion and parts of Dyfed, and thereby brought a large part of the ancient kingdom of Deheubarth under his control. He captured the castle of Cardigan, and on his borders he probably built or rebuilt the castles of Llandovery, Rhayader, and Nevern. He was certainly willing to chastise lesser princes for misdeeds. But his conquests were tempered by good sense, and were often consolidated by negotiating judicious marriage settlements. In this way Rhys bound to himself the native rulers of upland Glamorgan, Gwent and Brycheiniog. He also married two of his daughters to the Norman lords of Cemais, a policy culminating in the marriage of his son and heir, Gruffudd ap Rhys (d. 1201), to Matilda (d. 1210), a daughter of the powerful Anglo-Norman Marcher house of Braose.

So it was that Rhys secured the boundaries of his territory. His remarkable achievement in reversing the fortunes of his kingship cannot be underestimated. By 1180, Deheubarth had been reconstituted and was the premier Welsh kingdom, albeit under the overlordship of the English king.

Alas, centuries of rebuilding and repair prevent us from knowing what Lord Rhys's castle at Dinefwr looked like. Fundamentally, however, its layout may not have been dissimilar to that which survives today: the topography is ideally suited to the existing two-ward form. There may have been an inner 'ringwork' and an outer ward with two gates, and either a wooden or, more probably, a masonry defensive wall.

The Lord Rhys was a ruler of rare vision and talent who restored the fortunes of twelfth-century Deheubarth. As the figurehead of this ancient kingship, he was accorded burial in St Davids Cathedral, where this fourteenth-century tomb effigy lies.

Achievements of the Lord Rhys

Above: It is perhaps Strata Florida Abbey, with its striking west doorway, that best expresses the Lord Rhys's generous patronage of the religious life of Deheubarth.

Rhys was equally munificent in his patronage of the arts and in 1177 he held a festival of music and poetry at Cardigan. This contemporary manuscript illustration depicts a harpist (The National Library of Ireland, Ms. 700).

Rhys ap Gruffudd's achievements were founded upon his determined efforts — over a period of twenty years — to re-establish a stable Welsh dominion in Deheubarth after the ravages inflicted upon the area in the Norman period. Prolonged conflict with the Marcher lords and the Crown of England was finally terminated in 1171 when Henry II, at last reversing the aggressive policy he had hitherto pursued, recognized the position that Rhys had secured in Ystrad Tywi, Ceredigion, and parts of Dyfed. Their reconciliation meant that Henry was ensured the stability of Deheubarth at a time when he laboured with other major difficulties in Ireland and in his Continental possessions. Rhys's appointment as justiciar a year later — in charge of all aspects of royal administration in the region — demonstrated Henry's wish to gain the benefit of the prince's influence for peace in the Marcher areas, often where savage conflict continued. Rhys was able to take advantage of the peaceful and stable conditions in Deheubarth to consolidate the security of his dominion and promote its prosperity.

There are indications that he reformed the fiscal organization of his land. He may have been responsible for legal reform, for, although the earliest lawbook from Deheubarth dates from the thirteenth century, there are signs that an important revision of Welsh law was made in Rhys's time. There were, too, advances in religious and cultural life in the province. Rhys founded the Premonstratensian abbey of Talley; liberally endowed the Cistercian abbeys of Whitland and Strata Florida; planted a community of nuns at Llanllŷr; and supported the Hospitallers' house at Slebech and the Benedictine priory at Cardigan. In 1177, Rhys held a festival of poetry and music at Cardigan, which may be regarded as the first *eisteddfod*. A vibrant religious and cultural tradition is reflected in the poems of Gwynfardd Brycheiniog, possibly the court poet of Deheubarth, addressed to St David and to Rhys himself. Rhys's valour and his stature as a ruler of truly regal qualities are extolled in the eulogy by Cynddelw Brydydd Mawr and the grandiose Latin poem composed upon his death.

Rhys's success was achieved by virtue of eternal vigilance, a benign and shrewd good sense, and a certain amount of good fortune. It was never quite the same after the death of Henry II in 1189. With King Richard I (1189–99) relations were more difficult, and Rhys was forced to go on the offensive to counter new Anglo-Norman aggression in the Marcher territories. Rhys was also troubled by conflict among his sons who, several years before his death, anticipated the struggle for the succession. Rhys's campaigns in the Marcher lordships may well have been calculated to divert his sons' energies beyond the confines of his own territory. The problems that confronted him in his last years demonstrate that Deheubarth faced difficulties, which even Rhys's prodigious efforts could not resolve forever. He had reconstituted the kingdom of Deheubarth, and secured its status as a major Welsh province at a critical period in Anglo-Welsh relations. As Cynddelw wrote, Rhys had indeed restored 'the majesty of the south'.

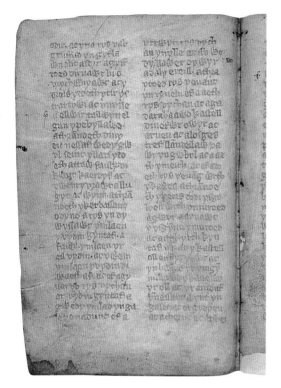

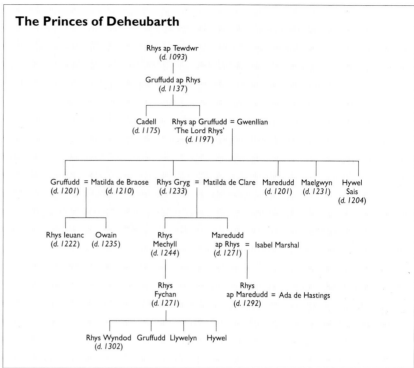

The Princes of Deheubarth

Rhys ap Tewdwr
(d. 1093)

Gruffudd ap Rhys
(d. 1137)

Cadell
(d. 1175)

Rhys ap Gruffudd = Gwenllian
'The Lord Rhys'
(d. 1197)

Gruffudd = Matilda de Braose   Rhys Gryg = Matilda de Clare   Maredudd   Maelgwyn   Hywel
(d. 1201)   (d. 1210)   (d. 1233)   (d. 1201)   (d. 1231)   Sais
                                                                                           (d. 1204)

Rhys Ieuanc   Owain   Rhys   Maredudd
(d. 1222)   (d. 1235)   Mechyll   ap Rhys = Isabel Marshal
                                 (d. 1244)   (d. 1271)

Rhys   Rhys
Fychan   ap Maredudd = Ada de Hastings
(d. 1271)   (d. 1292)

Rhys Wyndod   Gruffudd   Llywelyn   Hywel
(d. 1302)

The Princes of Deheubarth after the Lord Rhys

Following Rhys's death in 1197, his sons contested the succession to the kingdom of Deheubarth. Rhys had probably intended that his eldest legitimate son, Gruffudd ap Rhys (d. 1201), should inherit the kingdom, but his succession was challenged by two other sons, Maelgwyn ap Rhys (d. 1231) and Rhys Gryg (d. 1233). A vigorous struggle ensued, and castles were captured and recaptured in a period of prolonged conflict between the brothers, and — after the early death of Gruffudd — his sons, Rhys Ieuanc (d. 1222) and Owain (d. 1235). In one such encounter, in 1204, Maelgwyn lost the castles at Llandovery and Dinefwr —'the bolts and stays of all his territory' (*Brut y Tywysogyon*) — to his nephews, Rhys Ieuanc and Owain.

Almost ten years later, in 1213, the struggle continued as Rhys Gryg, another of the Lord Rhys's sons, was forced to defend Dinefwr against Rhys Ieuanc, who was again seeking to assert his claim to the inheritance. In the attack on the castle in January of that year, Rhys Ieuanc 'had ladders placed against the walls, and armed men to scale the walls'. On the first assault, the chronicler continued, 'the whole castle was taken except for the tower', though that, too, was surrendered before the afternoon.

The main beneficiaries of this tragic conflict within Deheubarth were outsiders. The English king, Anglo-Norman lords of the March and native Welsh neighbours, all took advantage until once again the days of independence seemed to be numbered. Finally, it was by the power of the prince of Gwynedd, Llywelyn ab Iorwerth (Llywelyn the Great), that a settlement was made. In 1216, he summoned the princes to Aberdyfi and induced them to accept a tripartite division of Deheubarth. Maelgwyn was to receive the south-west; the south-east, Ystrad Tywi (including Dinefwr and Dryslwyn), was to go to Rhys Gryg; and Rhys Ieuanc and Owain were to get Ceredigion. They were now all rulers by the grace of Llywelyn, diminished in stature and relegated to a lesser role in history. Deheubarth was never to recover the status it had enjoyed under the Lord Rhys. Despite this, it was in these decades that both castles achieved their mighty masonry constructions, before they were eventually lost to King Edward I.

Above left: In the struggle for succession to the kingdom of Deheubarth, Brut y Tywysogyon *tells how Rhys Ieuanc (d. 1222) had 'ladders placed against the walls, and armed men to scale the walls' at Dinefwr in 1213 (National Library of Wales, Peniarth Ms. 20).*

This early fourteenth-century manuscript illustration shows an attack on a castle using ladders and picks. Rhys Ieuanc may have mounted a similar operation when he attacked Dinefwr in 1213 (British Library Royal Ms. 10 E IV, f. 202).

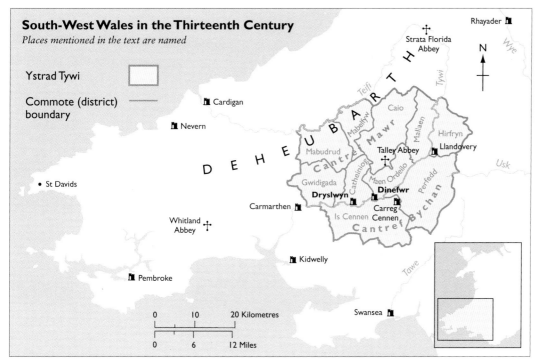

South-West Wales in the Thirteenth Century
Places mentioned in the text are named

Ystrad Tywi

Commote (district) boundary

In 1216, Llywelyn ab Iorwerth, the powerful prince of Gwynedd, imposed a tripartite division of Deheubarth on the squabbling heirs of the Lord Rhys. Thereafter the princes of Deheubarth were diminished in stature and relegated to a lesser role in history. This finely carved stone head, recovered from Llywelyn's castle at Degannwy in north Wales, may represent the prince himself (National Museum of Wales).

So it was that Rhys Gryg, 'the Hoarse', was confirmed in the possession of his father's castle of Dinefwr and lordship over Ystrad Tywi, and in 1219 his position was further strengthened by his marriage to Matilda de Clare, sister of Earl Gilbert (d. 1230) of Gloucester. Even so, Rhys could never take control of his estates for granted. As events unfolded, Llywelyn ab Iorwerth was to do homage to King Henry III in return for peace and for possession of the vital castles of Carmarthen and Cardigan, and he was requested to persuade 'all the magnates of the whole of Wales' to do the same. Rhys steadfastly refused. It was only when Llywelyn brought an army south, leading to a skirmish between the forces of Gwynedd and Deheubarth at Carmarthen bridge, that Rhys finally yielded.

In his 1220 letter to the king (p. 4), Llywelyn refers to Rhys dismantling the fortification of Dinefwr in expectation of his coming. How significant this really was we can only guess. But thereafter, for thirteen relatively peaceful years, Rhys lived until his death as a vassal of the king and an adherent of Llywelyn. He had the time, and perhaps the opportunity, to rebuild afresh.

On Rhys Gryg's death in 1233, his territory of Ystrad Tywi was to be divided. His elder son, Rhys Mechyll (d. 1244), inherited Dinefwr and the east of Ystrad Tywi, while the younger, Maredudd ap Rhys

(d. 1271), succeeded to the west, probably ruling from Dryslwyn. In 1240, both did homage to Henry III (Maredudd travelled to Westminster while Rhys, a few days later, journeyed to Windsor), but now as tenants-in-chief of the king, freed of their subordination to the house of Gwynedd by Llywelyn's death in 1240. Rhys Mechyll was succeeded by his son Rhys Fychan (d. 1271). He and his uncle Maredudd were to side with Llywelyn's son, Dafydd, in his attempt to re-establish native control over the whole of Wales, but the efforts collapsed with Dafydd's death in 1246. Rhys Fychan's punishment was the loss of Dinefwr to the English for a short time, though he was re-established there by 1248 when he agreed to recognize the jurisdiction of the king's court at Carmarthen. Meanwhile, Maredudd had been allowed to keep Dryslwyn.

It is from this time, in 1246, that we have the first reliable documentary reference to Dryslwyn Castle, despite the fact that the recently excavated evidence suggests that it must have been in existence for some years before. The source in question, the native Latin chronicle, *Annales Cambrie*, makes passing mention of a siege at the castle by the seneschal of Carmarthen on behalf of its 'rightful owner'. But we are given no indication of the outcome, or, indeed, who the chronicler considered its rightful owner to be.

Opposite: The keep and adjacent Welsh gate at Dinefwr are thought to represent works undertaken by Rhys Gryg. Certainly, during the years of relative peace between 1220 and his death in 1233, Rhys Gryg may have had the opportunity to embark on building operations of this scale. This fourteenth-century tomb effigy of Rhys Gryg lies in the cathedral church at St Davids.

A view of Dinefwr Castle from the south. Medieval texts accorded the castle special status as the principal seat of the kingship of Deheubarth.

The Development of Dinefwr Castle

There is nothing in the surviving archaeological evidence to argue for or against there having been a fortification on the site before the time of the Lord Rhys, and the present defensive layout was probably first adopted in his time. By the later twelfth century, two enclosures stood side by side along the rock crag, defined on the three open sides by a deep rock-cut ditch. Buildings within the defences would have been of timber or stone, but their form remains unknown.

It seems unlikely that so eminent a personage as the Lord Rhys would not have wished to embellish and strengthen his principal stronghold, especially since he is known to have rebuilt the castle at Cardigan, and possibly that at Nevern, in stone. Perhaps it was Rhys who constructed the first masonry curtain wall at Dinefwr, possibly with a now lost stone tower. By the time of the siege of 1213 (p. 7), there were certainly walls and a tower strong enough to withstand siege engines, and there is no contemporary mention of the castle being burnt. It might have been a section of this primary wall which Rhys Gryg dismantled to placate Prince Llywelyn in 1220.

The great circular keep belongs to a group of similar structures, such as those at Bronllys, Skenfrith and Tretower (as well as at Dryslwyn), most of which are conventionally dated to around the 1230s. At Dinefwr, the keep and the adjacent Welsh gate may have been the work of Rhys Gryg, who held considerable influence, and — for the last thirteen years of his life — presided over a period of relative peace, during which he may have had the opportunity to embark on building operations of this scale. He also held the lands around Dryslwyn, and the similar overall plan, the style of the keep,

and the entrance arrangements there, are all probably too close to be merely coincidental. After his death in 1233, Rhys's lands were held by different branches of the Deheubarth dynasty.

Following the Edwardian conquest, documentary sources reveal that repairs were carried out on the tower, bridge, hall and 'little tower'; a new gate was constructed, and the ditches were cleaned and extended around the town. Also, two large and three small buildings were erected in the bailey. It is probable, therefore, that the keep had been damaged and needed repair; the 'little tower' may refer to the north-west tower which seems to have been remodelled at this time. It might also have been during this phase that the rectangular chamber block on the north-east was constructed, perhaps adapting an earlier structure which had previously acted as a hall. The new block projected beyond the line of the northern curtain wall, and was equipped with a watch turret, and may — for a short time — have served as both hall and apartments, until the replacement hall on the west was added. The new gate mentioned among the repairs of the 1280s may have been an extensive remodelling of the entrance passage, creating an inner gate and gate-passage from the original gatehouse, which was itself extended outwards, thereby necessitating the redigging of the defensive ditch. It seems likely that the southern turret was constructed as part of the new gate arrangements.

Somewhat later, the rectangular hall was built alongside the chamber block, again protruding beyond the curtain wall. This addition, coupled with the raising of another structure along the western curtain, made the entrance to the north-west tower very cramped. By this stage, accommodation and

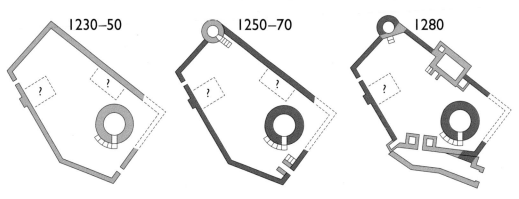

1230–50   1250–70   1280

comfort were evidently considered to be important. The hall, the western building, and the remodelling of the windows of the rectangular chamber block may all date to the years after 1326, when considerable sums were spent on the castle during the Hakeluts' custody (p. 19). The insertion of the ground-floor entrance in the keep may also date from this time.

Thereafter, additions were probably few, though we have frequent records of the poor state of repair of different sections of the castle, such as in 1343 and 1353 when the great keep was reported to be on the verge of collapse. After the Glyn Dŵr siege, new building and repairs were apparently undertaken, and it may have been at this period that the crenellated south wall on the entrance passage was totally rebuilt to butt up against the south turret. There are no records of work at Dinefwr for the remainder of the Middle Ages, and it appears that from the fifteenth century the old site was abandoned in favour of the more convenient situation of the first Newton House.

The castle was transformed in the late seventeenth century when the top of the keep was rebuilt to form a summerhouse. The southern turret was also equipped with a roof and a tiled floor, and the castle became the focus for summer visits and picnics. The earthworks surrounding the castle were altered somewhat to allow easier access from Newton House. By the late eighteenth century, however, both roofs had been destroyed by fire and the castle was largely abandoned to nature. During periodic repairs by the Dynevor Estate through to the twentieth century, large areas of walling were rebuilt or refaced, efforts which occasionally make full understanding of the medieval work difficult. Even so, this earlier conservation undoubtedly contributed to the survival of the remarkably intact little inner ward.

Above: An artist's impression of how the castle and surrounding town of Dinefwr may have appeared during the years after 1326, when considerable sums had been spent on the castle during the Hakeluts' custody (Illustration by Chris Jones-Jenkins, 1999).

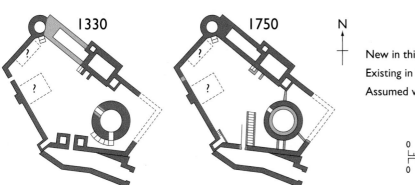

1330   1750   N

New in this phase
Existing in this phase
Assumed walls

0   10   20 Metres
0   30   60 Feet

The Development of Dryslwyn Castle

Castell y Bere, established by Prince Llywelyn ab Iorwerth in 1221, stretches along the summit of a remote rocky outcrop in the Dysynni valley. Like Dinefwr and Dryslwyn, it was equipped with a strong tower and a defended ward, the size and shape of which was dictated by its hilltop location.

The earliest castle at Dryslwyn was probably raised during the second quarter of the thirteenth century. The buildings included the round tower or keep, with an adjoining polygonal ward enclosed with a curtain wall, and with a simple gateway entrance on the north-east side. Inside this castle there was a single large hall — the great hall — with open ground and bedrock to the north, and a small cluster of wooden buildings to the east. South of the hall was a small stone building, probably a kitchen, with a hearth. In the north-west corner, between the great hall and the curtain wall, another small structure was probably used as a prison.

Many early Welsh castles are of similar form, perched in defensible positions high on hilltops, overlooking valleys, with a strong tower and a defended ward whose size and shape were dictated by the size and shape of the hilltop. Indeed, the similarity between the layout of Dryslwyn and that of Dinefwr, in particular, reinforces the idea that their initial plans were conceived by the same Welsh prince.

There were many additions to the castle in the years that followed. In the mid-thirteenth century, a second (middle) ward was added to the north and east of the initial defences, virtually doubling the overall size of the stronghold. Meanwhile, in the inner ward, a new great chamber was built to the east of the earlier great hall. Subsequently, it was almost certainly Rhys ap Maredudd (d. 1292) who further enlarged and improved the castle in the 1280s. Rhys had been rewarded for his loyalty to the Crown in the war of 1282–83, and it was probably the wealth derived from his new lands which enabled him to invest in the extensive building programme at Dryslwyn.

Within the inner ward, substantial walls were raised overlooking the Tywi; the great hall (later described as the 'King's Hall') was remodelled; a series of apartments was built adjoining the great hall, with a projecting chapel tower at the eastern end; and there was a newly mortared courtyard at the centre of the complex. Alongside this work, Rhys also added a third (outer) ward to the castle. All in all, by 1287, Rhys had made Dryslwyn one

Early/Mid-Thirteenth Century: Phase I

Mid-Thirteenth Century: Phase II

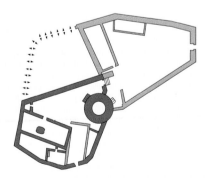

0   15 Metres

0   50 Feet

N

Late Thirteenth Century

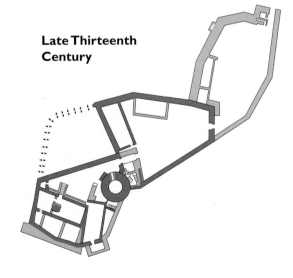

New in this phase

Existing in this phase

Left: The southern walls of the apartment block and the chapel are the most prominent sections of masonry that remain standing at Dryslwyn Castle (David Robinson).

Below: A reconstruction of Dryslwyn Castle as it may have appeared during the early thirteenth century, prior to the addition of the middle ward. The stone buildings included the round keep, the great hall and a kitchen (Illustration by Chris Jones-Jenkins, 1999).

of the largest masonry castles ever raised by native Welsh lords, a structure impressive enough to rival any number of strongholds raised by Anglo-Norman and English lords of the March.

During the ensuing English occupation, although there was much repair work undertaken from time to time, there was very little new building.

The castle was very deliberately decommissioned in the earlier fifteenth century. The passage through the outer, or main, gatehouse was walled up, and access into the basement of the round tower was also blocked. The site was then looted, with hinges taken from the main doors, and even the stone treads removed from steps. All in all, this meant Dryslwyn could no longer be used as an effective front-line stronghold. The actions were very probably carried out by the English forces which retook the castle following its surrender to Owain Glyn Dŵr in 1403. The intention was presumably to prevent the site being held by any hostile forces in future years.

At a later date, the castle was deliberately put to the torch, with very extensive archaeological evidence to show that all the major buildings were burnt to the ground. Demolition of the upstanding walls followed, apart from the two prominent sections on the south side.

This imaginative illustration of King Edward I (1272–1307) attended by Llywelyn ap Gruffudd, prince of Wales (d. 1282), appears in a sixteenth-century manuscript. Llywelyn continued to influence the balance of power in Deheubarth, as Llywelyn ab Iorwerth had done, but ultimately it was his failure to pay homage to the king that provoked Edward's invasion of Wales in 1277 (The Royal Library, Wriothesley Ms. quire B; The Royal Collection © 2006, Her Majesty Queen Elizabeth II).

The Rise of Llywelyn ap Gruffudd

During the next twenty-five years Ystrad Tywi came under the influence of Llywelyn ab Iorwerth's grandson, Llywelyn ap Gruffudd (d. 1282), his opportunity to intervene reflecting the political situation in the area. Relations between Rhys Fychan and Maredudd were strained, probably because of continuing disputes over the extent of the territories that they ruled. Securing aid from the royal

commander at Carmarthen, Rhys Fychan had the better of Maredudd, who thereupon identified himself with the cause of Llywelyn. Late in 1256, with Maredudd at his side, Llywelyn invaded Ystrad Tywi and ousted Rhys Fychan entirely. Thus Maredudd became lord of the whole of Ystrad Tywi. In desperation, Rhys Fychan turned to the king's commander, Stephen Bauzan, who led an army into the Tywi valley to restore Rhys's authority. At a critical point in the advance to Dinefwr, somewhere near Llandeilo Fawr, Rhys Fychan deserted, and the royal army suffered a devastating defeat at Cymerau. By the summer of 1257, almost the whole of south-west Wales was in Welsh hands, placing even the great lordship of Pembroke under threat.

Llywelyn now sought reconciliation with Rhys Fychan and Maredudd. The territorial settlement he envisaged meant that Dinefwr and much of the adjoining territory of Ystrad Tywi was restored to Rhys Fychan, Maredudd being confined to a rather restricted lordship centred on Dryslwyn. Disillusioned by the fact that his adherence to Llywelyn had not won him the benefits expected, Maredudd returned to the king's fealty. Llywelyn responded by taking him captive and formally convicted him of disloyalty in 1258; he was imprisoned at Criccieth Castle. Although he was released three years later, relations with Llywelyn were permanently soured.

When, by the Treaty of Montgomery in 1267, King Henry III granted Llywelyn, now prince of Wales, the allegiance of all the other princes of Wales, Maredudd's homage was specifically denied. Three years later, in 1270, Henry agreed to Llywelyn's wish that he be granted Maredudd's homage upon payment of 5,000 marks (£3,300) — a huge sum in the money of the day. The king was persuaded to do so by his son, Edward, who wished to use the money to meet the expenses of the crusade on which he was about to embark. Once again, the princes of south-west Wales ruled only with the agreement of the house of Gwynedd.

A year later, in August 1271, Maredudd died 'in his own castle at Dryslwyn' and was buried at Whitland Abbey, and just three weeks later Rhys Fychan died 'in his own castle at Dinefwr' and was buried at Talley Abbey. Rhys's son, Rhys Wyndod (d. 1302), succeeded to Dinefwr. At the same time, Dryslwyn and associated lands passed to Maredudd's son, Rhys ap Maredudd (d. 1292).

Edward I's Conquest of Wales: The Castles under English Rule

The reverse of the great seal of Edward I. Although the king received the submission of the two Deheubarth princes, Rhys ap Maredudd (d. 1292) and Rhys Wyndod (d. 1302), in the summer of 1277, when the Welsh cause crumbled, his failure to reward them properly eventually led to further rebellion (The National Archives: PRO).

On the death of King Henry in 1272, Edward I came to the English throne and within little more than a decade he had destroyed the power of the prince of Wales. His patience exhausted by Llywelyn's repeated defiance, Edward ordered Payn de Chaworth (d. 1279) to assemble an army at Carmarthen. Resistance in the south crumbled rapidly in the summer of 1277. Rhys ap Maredudd was the first to seek terms and was allowed to retain Dryslwyn and the commotes (districts) of Catheiniog and Mabudrud (see map p. 9). Within a month, Rhys Wyndod had also deserted Llywelyn and submitted to the king. He was reinstated in the majority of his castles and lands, but he was not allowed to retain the symbolic seat of Dinefwr. It was confiscated by the king, and was placed in the custody of the justiciar of west Wales, Bogo de Knovil.

Both princes had reason to feel aggrieved by the treatment they had received. Rhys ap Maredudd resented the fact that his early submission to the king in the war of 1277, which had proved of great benefit to the English campaign, had not been better rewarded. Rhys Wyndod faced a new predicament, for he was now confronted with legal action brought before the royal justices by John Giffard, now lord of Llandovery, who claimed part of the Welsh prince's inheritance. Rhys ap Maredudd adhered to King Edward, but Rhys Wyndod, angered by his treatment in the judicial proceedings and resentful of the king's failure to secure him justice, had reasons of his own to join the rebellion initiated by Dafydd ap Gruffudd (d. 1283), brother of the prince of Wales, in spring 1282. Forced to yield to royal forces, who were now able to use Dinefwr as a base for their operations in Ystrad Tywi, Rhys Wyndod finally forfeited his inheritance. He was exiled to Gwynedd, along with several other princes of Deheubarth and Powys. He lived to see first the death of Llywelyn ap Gruffudd in combat near Builth in December 1282, and then Dafydd's capture and execution, before he himself was sent to the Tower of London for perpetual imprisonment.

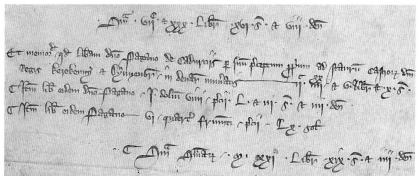

Above: Detail of a document recording the payment of £285 10s to Payn de Chaworth (d. 1279) in 1277. The account refers to the provision and repair of Edward I's newly acquired castles of Dinefwr and Carreg Cennen (The National Archives: PRO, E 101/3/20).

Left: This manuscript illustration depicts the death of Llywelyn ap Gruffudd, which took place at a skirmish near Builth Wells in December 1282. Following his death, Rhys Wyndod was imprisoned in the Tower of London having finally forfeited Dinefwr (British Library, Cotton Nero Ms. D II, f. 182).

A view of Dryslwyn from the west. On or about 15 August 1287, an English army of over 11,000 men assembled on the flat valley floor in front of the Welsh stronghold and the siege of Dryslwyn Castle began.

In the aftermath, Rhys ap Maredudd of Dryslwyn, now the only descendant of the Lord Rhys left with some degree of power and one of the few Welsh princes to have remained loyal to the Crown, was rewarded with territory. But he was again denied Dinefwr, and in 1283 was required to acknowledge that he had no rights to the stronghold. A year later, by the Statute of Wales, Edward I ordained a new system of government for the Crown lands in Wales. His measures included the provision for the consolidation of his authority in the south-western counties of Carmarthen and Cardigan, already created by his predecessor.

Rhys ap Maredudd was soon involved in a series of bitter disputes with Robert de Tibetot, the new justiciar of west Wales (1281–98). The situation rapidly worsened, and in June 1287 Rhys suddenly

attacked and captured the castles of Dinefwr, Carreg Cennen and Llandovery. The constables were slaughtered, and many defenders left for dead. The English response was swift and immensely powerful (p. 17). A great army of over 11,000 men was raised in various parts of England and Wales and they marched to Carmarthen to assemble under the king's cousin, Earl Edmund of Cornwall (d. 1300). From here, in the second week of August, they set out to lay siege to Dryslwyn Castle, where Rhys had established his defensive headquarters. This siege is particularly well known because of the relative abundance of documentation. The castle fell after three weeks, during which time Dinefwr had also been retaken. Rhys himself fled, but after a few more years of resistance he was captured in April 1292 and executed at York for treason.

The 1287 Siege of Dryslwyn Castle

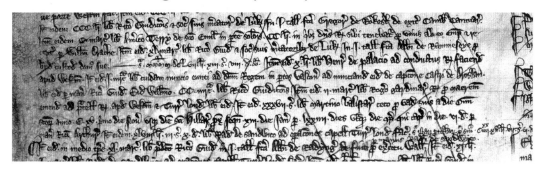

Left: Upon the culmination of the three-week siege of Dryslwyn, a messenger was despatched post-haste to Edward I, away in Gascony at the time, with the news of the castle's capture. This contemporary manuscript records the events (The National Archives: PRO, E 403/55).

In the wake of Rhys ap Maredudd's revolt of 1287, there was a swift, well-coordinated, and effective English reaction. With Edward I out of the country, it was left to his regent in England, Earl Edmund of Cornwall, to take the lead. A great army was to be assembled at Carmarthen; on 16 July writs were sent to the lords of the March to raise their forces.

On 9 August, Earl Edmund set out from Carmarthen for Rhys's castle at Dryslwyn, at the head of an army of some 4,000 men. Some of these had been raised in England; others had been assembled locally under Robert de Tibetot. On 15 August, the earl's force was joined by an army of 6,700 ranks and officers, gathered under Reginald Grey (d. 1308), who had set out from Chester, and Roger l'Estrange (d. 1311) who had marched from Montgomery.

With the combined force of more than 11,000 assembled on the flat valley floor in front of Dryslwyn, on or just after 15 August, the siege of Dryslwyn Castle began. Many of the men coming from Chester were drawn from the building works on King Edward's north Wales castles. These craftsmen and others constructed a trébuchet, a siege machine capable of hurling huge stones at the castle walls. This machine, constructed with timber, hides, rope and lead, cost £14. A total of twenty quarrymen and twenty-four carters were employed to shape and move the large stone balls that were hurled by the trébuchet at the castle.

In addition, the besiegers were attempting to undermine the castle walls. Tradition records that they brought down a large section near the projecting chapel block, but archaeological evidence suggests that it was on the other side of the castle, facing the town. The mining was marred by the collapse of a wall, crushing to death a group of nobles who were

inspecting the work, including Nicholas, baron de Stafford, Sir William de Monte Caniso (Montchensey) and Sir John de Bonvillars. The castle was captured by 5 September, and, although Rhys ap Maredudd escaped, his wife and son were captured. The siege undoubtedly caused damage to the castle, and repairs were carried out shortly afterwards (p. 18).

The archaeological excavation of the site has produced important evidence from the time of this siege (pp. 46–47). Two substantial stone balls, over 16 inches (40cm) in diameter, thrown by the trébuchet, were recovered. Also recovered were many smaller stones, which were thrown at the castle, as well as links of chain mail, arrowheads, slingshots and a spearhead. Over one hundred arrowheads were recovered, many with long sharp points deliberately made to penetrate armour and chain mail.

A great siege engine was constructed in preparation for the attack on Dryslwyn by Edward I's forces. This near-contemporary manuscript illustration shows soldiers in combat and a stone-throwing engine in use (© Photo SCALA, Florence — Pierpont Morgan Library, New York, Ms. 638, f. 23v).

Above: Following the siege of Dryslwyn, minor works were undertaken at the castle. In a set of accounts for 1287–89 a payment of £109 was listed for carpenters, smiths and charcoal burners engaged in the construction of a new mill. This early fourteenth-century manuscript illustration shows carpenters at work sawing great timbers (British Library, Royal Ms. 10 E IV, f. 99v).

Right: An artist's impression of the town and castle of Dryslwyn as they may have appeared in the late thirteenth or early fourteenth century (Illustration by Chris Jones-Jenkins, 1999).

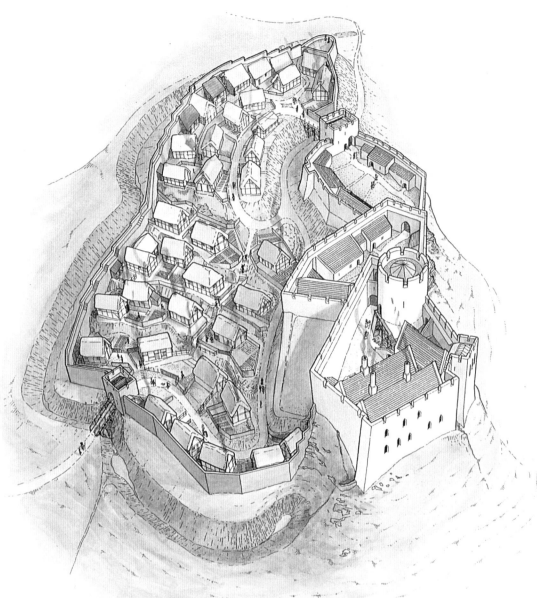

Dinefwr and Dryslwyn as Castles of the English Crown

From 1287 Dinefwr and Dryslwyn were to serve as royal castles in the custody of a constable of the Crown. Records, which survive from the ensuing years, provide us with some indication of the fate of the buildings at each site. At Dryslwyn, for example, in a set of accounts for 1287–89, the constable, Alan de Plucknet, listed a payment of almost £130 made to masons and quarrymen involved with repairs after the siege. A further £109 went to carpenters, smiths and charcoal burners engaged in the construction of a new mill, and £36 was paid for the felling of woods around the castle, the renovation of the ditches, and for various other minor works-related items. Interestingly, at Dinefwr the recorded expenditure on repairs was somewhat smaller, with only £59 13s. 6d. spent in the period to 1290.

The accounts enrolled by the justiciar of west Wales around the turn of the century paint a vivid picture of life in these military outposts. Supplies of commodities such as grain, beef, honey, salt and wine had to be bought in the surrounding area and transported across country to feed the standing garrisons, each of twenty-four men under a constable. Minor repairs were sometimes needed, such as the essential work carried out to the roofs of houses within the castles after 'the great wind' in January 1300. And, from 1303–04, we read of an armourer employed for three weeks in 'burnishing and mending the iron armour' held at both fortresses.

For much of the 1290s, Dinefwr had been held by John Giffard (d. 1299), but in 1310–11 the castle, town and demesne lands were granted to Edmund Hakelut for life, and he was later able to secure the constableship for his son, another Edmund (d. 1360). This comparatively long period of tenure by a single family was interrupted in 1317 when Edward II (1307–27) gave both Dinefwr and Dryslwyn to his unscrupulous favourite, Hugh Despenser the younger (d. 1326).

Dinefwr, already seriously damaged by fire during a widespread Welsh revolt in 1316, was one of the Despenser castles which suffered from further attack — this time by outraged Marcher lords — in 1321. Considerable sums were spent on repairs to the buildings after the site was returned to the elder Edmund Hakelut following Despenser's fall in 1326. Meanwhile, at Dryslwyn, where a new wooden-framed granary and a stone bakehouse had been built in 1306, the attacks of 1321 had again presumably led to extensive damage. Some years later, in 1338–39, major repairs to the block of rooms on the west side of the 'King's Hall', said to be 'entirely decayed ... and fallen to the ground', were recorded. At the same time, modifications were made to the hall itself, including a new window and doorway. Elsewhere in the castle attention was paid to 'other defects of the walls, towers and turrets'.

In a survey of 1343 undertaken for Edward, the Black Prince (d. 1376), it was reported that the great tower at Dinefwr was on the point of collapse, and it was estimated that £139 would be required to effect repairs. And, despite the repairs and modifications of 1338–39, Dryslwyn appears to have been in an even poorer state. The Black Prince's inspectors gave a figure of £341 needed for fresh works, especially the restoration of the inner bailey wall, the 'great tower', the 'tower at the end of the hall in the middle of the castle', and the 'tower called Appeltour'.

At neither site, however, are there records of any large-scale rebuilding carried out on the defences in the later fourteenth century. There are reports of new service rooms, bakehouses and the like, but the inescapable conclusion is that the castles were becoming neglected. Though they were kept intact and reasonably comfortable by their custodians, the major centres of royal authority and power in the south-west were now irrefutably at Carmarthen and Cardigan.

At the beginning of the fifteenth century, a new champion of Welsh hopes and ambitions, Owain Glyn Dŵr, gave the English keepers of the castles in south-west Wales cause to regret any complacency. In the early summer of 1403 Glyn Dŵr himself arrived in the Tywi valley; the various royal servants found themselves in a desperate plight. Writing from Carreg Cennen, for example, John Skidmore described how he pleaded with Glyn Dŵr, during their meeting at Dryslwyn, for a safe conduct for the women folk in his entourage, but he had to report that Glyn Dŵr 'wolde none graunte me'. In the event, the constable left to defend Dryslwyn, Rhys ap Gruffudd, surrendered to the rebels on 4 July.

A new champion of Welsh hopes and ambitions, Owain Glyn Dŵr, arrived in the Tywi valley in the summer of 1403. The constable of Dryslwyn, Rhys ap Gruffudd, surrendered the castle to the rebels on 4 July. The arms of Glyn Dŵr appear on this harness decoration found at Harlech Castle (National Museum of Wales).

In his letter to the receiver at Brecon in July 1403, John Skidmore, constable of Carreg Cennen, recorded how he met with Owain Glyn Dŵr at Dryslwyn to plead for the safe conduct home of his mother-in-law and wife (British Library, Cotton Cleopatra, F III, f. 153).

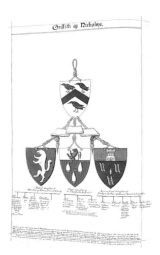

The arms of Gruffudd ap Nicholas (d. 1460), together with those of his three wives, from a Dinefwr pedigree book probably compiled in the nineteenth century. It may have been Gruffudd who built the first Newton House at Dinefwr (By kind permission of Lord Dynevor/ Carmarthenshire Archive Service, Dynevor Additional Ms. 73, f. 17b).

Above: Although he contributed to the maintenance of Newton House, following his appointment as justiciar of south Wales, Sir Rhys ap Thomas (d. 1525) devoted much energy and resources to his newly acquired residence of Carew Castle, Pembrokeshire.

Right: The tomb effigy of Sir Rhys ap Thomas, resting in St Peter's Church, Carmarthen. Dinefwr was one of the many rewards granted to Sir Rhys by King Henry VII (1485–1509) for his loyal support at the end of the Wars of the Roses.

Meanwhile, from 2 July, a force led by Henry Don, his son and Gwilym ap Philip, had taken up siege positions at Dinefwr. On 7 July, the constable, John (or Jankyn) Havard — 'writing in haste and in dread' — said that if no relief was forthcoming he would have no option but to abandon the castle by night and flee to the safety of Brecon. Yet remarkably the embattled and isolated garrison held on, resisting furious assault. Both sides were doubtless aware of the potent symbolism of the site as 'the chief place in old time', and neither was prepared to yield readily. Finally, after ten days of action, it was the besieging army that was forced to withdraw.

Following the revolt at large, it was some three years before English authority was re-established in the Tywi valley. By 1409, £89 was being spent on repairs to Dinefwr and on the construction of new buildings there. At Dryslwyn, on the other hand, the Glyn Dŵr episode may have led to the final abandonment of the castle. No records of any repairs survive, and it is not known to have played any part in later military activity. Indeed, archaeological excavation suggests that it was deliberately demolished sometime in the first half of the fifteenth century.

After this period of disturbance, new constables were appointed to Dinefwr, first Hugh Standish in 1408, and then his brother, Christopher, in 1411. After the death of the latter in 1425, his son, Roland, was appointed. A senior military figure much engaged with foreign wars, Sir Roland Standish (d. 1435) effectively passed the responsibility for the running of the castle to Gruffudd ap Nicholas (d. 1460).

The descendant of a notable Welsh family, Gruffudd was described in a seventeenth-century biography as 'infinitely subtle and crafty, ambitious beyond measure'. He rose rapidly in power and influence, gaining the trust of busy officials who then used him to deputize for their administrative duties. He gradually acquired extensive landholdings in Carmarthenshire and Cardiganshire and had great influence in local government. In fact, it may have been Gruffudd who built the first Newton House at Dinefwr, as the comfortable home of a gentleman away from the gaunt grimness of the medieval castle. Eventually, as a Lancastrian supporter, Gruffudd found his power curbed on the outbreak of the Wars of the Roses (1455–85). In 1456, he was deprived of the castle, town and lands of

Dinefwr — one of his most cherished grants. He was to die four years later.

The castle was later returned to Gruffudd ap Nicholas's family, his descendants continuing to hold the estate, except for three brief periods, until the present day. Gruffudd's principal heir, Thomas, apparently lived at Abermarlais, the family home of his rich wife, Elizabeth. His son, the famous Rhys ap Thomas (d. 1525), was a stout supporter of Henry Tudor, assisting him with his invasion at Milford Haven, and he was knighted for his services at Bosworth Field in 1485.

Sir Rhys secured control of Dinefwr for life, with the stronghold evidently still a symbol of some significance, linking him with its glorious history. He became justiciar of south Wales, acting as the equivalent of the king's viceroy. His favour outlived King Henry VII (1485–1509) and, in turn, Henry VIII (1509–47) kept 'good Father Ris' in his position of authority. Though his main residence was at Abermarlais, Sir Rhys definitely maintained the house at Dinefwr (Newton). Meanwhile, one can only assume, the old castle itself continued its slow decline to picturesque ruin.

The Picturesque and the Later History of the Castles

By the later eighteenth century, both Dinefwr and Dryslwyn had become examples of those ivy-clad ruins so beloved by the Romantics. Artists and tourists who travelled across Britain at the time were moved by the aesthetic concept of the Picturesque, defined by William Gilpin as 'that peculiar kind of beauty which is agreeable in a picture'. In particular, they favoured scenes where wrought wild nature combined with parkscape, or where ruinous and rustic architectural fragments were juxtaposed with the great house to combine into a 'beauteous whole'. Newton House,

with its formal garden, undulating wooded park and the nearby ruined castle, formed an ideal subject.

Even so, monuments might always be improved, and it was decided to attempt just this at Dinefwr. The intention was in part to improve upon the silhouette of the castle, whilst also providing a comfortable lookout point by the addition of a summerhouse. Precisely when the extraordinary summerhouse was added to the great round tower is unknown, but it does appear in some of the earliest recorded depictions of the site. Three of a series of four paintings, thought to date to the late seventeenth century, show the addition quite clearly, as does the 1740 engraving of the castle by Samuel and Nathaniel Buck (p. 22). It was doubtless in much the same period that a small turret on the south wall

One of a series of four paintings of the Dynevor Estate, dating to around 1660. This is perhaps the earliest depiction of the medieval castle showing the great round tower capped with its extraordinary summerhouse (National Trust).

The addition of the summerhouse can be seen clearly in Samuel and Nathaniel Buck's 1740 engraving of Dinefwr. The castle is shown from the east (National Library of Wales).

Opposite: Llandeilo Bridge and Dinevor Castle, *painted in 1796 by J. M. W. Turner (1775–1851). Like much of Turner's work, the artist juxtaposes images of past and present to convey a sense of the ultimate frailty of human endeavour (National Museum of Wales).*

adjacent to the gate was roofed and plastered internally. It had a window looking south over the river valley, while the higher main summerhouse had large windows giving panoramic views in all directions, including the parkland between the castle and the mansion. In 1775, George Rice (d. 1779) commissioned Lancelot 'Capability' Brown (1716–83) to provide advice on landscaping. Some of the earthworks at the entrance to the old castle are probably the result of such landscaping and may have been intended to provide a suitable disembarking point for visitors.

By the time John 'Warwick' Smith (d. 1831) visited Dinefwr in 1796–97, the summerhouse had been destroyed by fire, and his picture shows it with ruinous upper parts. Although the magnificent landscape painted by J. M. W. Turner (d. 1851) barely shows the castle in any detail, its concentration upon the ruinous bridge — with the almost ghost-like features of the ancient fortress in the distance — very much reflects the contemporary attitude towards the frailty of human achievement. Finally, an aquatint of 1779 by Paul Sandby (d. 1809) in some ways exemplifies the ideal of the Picturesque (p. 40). The jagged outline of the castle contrasts with the peaceful foreground of landscaped park with cattle, deer, and an aristocratic figure on horseback.

Dryslwyn does not seem to have enjoyed the same popularity as a subject for artists in search of

the Picturesque, perhaps because its early abandonment and collapse made it a much less conspicuous landscape feature. Nevertheless, it was evidently a popular site for picnicking parties during the eighteenth and nineteenth centuries, as the presence of porcelain fragments excavated from around the gatehouse testifies.

Apart from artists, contemporary writers and poets also went in search of the Picturesque. One early example was John Dyer, whose poem 'Grongar Hill' (1738) describes Dinefwr's 'old green tow'r, whose battered brow/frowns upon the vale below', while a tour account of 1794 by V. Sotheby speaks of the 'ivied battlements' of 'ancient Dinevawr'.

After the heyday of the travelling artists and writers, which lasted until about 1830, interest in the ruins of Dinefwr and Dryslwyn lessened. Neglect led to further collapse, and gradually to a general smothering with debris, trees and undergrowth. Even so, periodic repairs were carried out at Dinefwr by the owners of the estate until the present century.

The remains at Dryslwyn were taken into the guardianship of the State in 1980, and a comprehensive programme of archaeological excavation and conservation followed over the next fifteen years. Conservation and consolidation of the ruins at Dinefwr began slightly later. Both sites are now maintained by Cadw.

A Tour of Dinefwr Castle

The walk to the old castle of Dinefwr starts from the car park at Newton House. From here, there are various signed footpaths to the castle through the parklands of the Dinefwr Estate. The routes are shown on the adjacent map and further details can be obtained from the National Trust visitor centre. This apparently natural landscape is the product of careful work in the seventeenth, eighteenth and nineteenth centuries, when the old castle was seen as a Picturesque feature — a Romantic ruin enticing visitors, who might be staying at Newton House, to climb to the ancient ivy-clad walls. Walking along the footpaths, you follow the routes that those early travellers climbed, equipped with their sketch pads or writing materials to record their impressions of this celebrated place.

As the paths wind uphill, the castle appears intermittently on the skyline and you soon enter woodland. The woodland has remained largely undisturbed and this is reflected in the rich diversity of plants and insects. This variety in turn provides a food source for the many bird species, which breed here, as well as the many animals that frequent the woods. In view of this importance to wildlife the area has been designated a Site of Special Scientific Interest (SSSI) by the Nature Conservancy Council.

Signposts will take you to a track, which brings you into the castle in the manner of the medieval traveller, along the gentle approach from the east, through the outer defences and gate, and on through the outer ward towards the main gate of the castle.

From the outer ward, you may care to follow the route suggested below; alternatively, you may choose to explore the castle for yourself using the bird's-eye view at the front of the guidebook and the ground plan on the inside back cover.

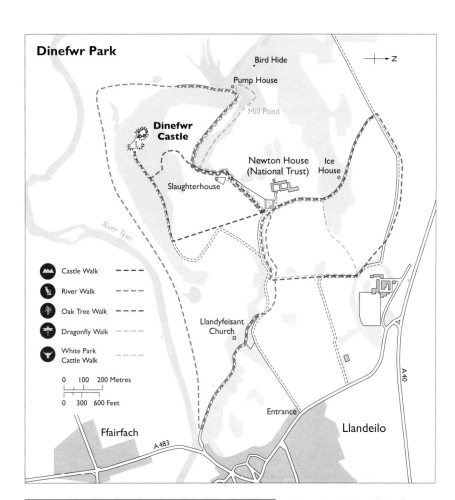

From the gravel car park a rural path of grass and gravel leads through the estate to the castle hill. A steep path, with steps in places, leads up to the castle. There is a steep ramp through the gatehouse. Inside the castle the ward is mainly level. Some rooms and the wall-walks are up stone steps, some without handrails. There is an accessible car-parking space near the castle on a track through several farm gates. The National Trust custodian can provide information on how to get to the accessible bay.

Opposite: A view of Dinefwr Castle looking across the parkland of the Dinefwr Estate from the north-east. This is perhaps one of the aspects enjoyed by earlier visitors in search of the Picturesque.

The outer ward at Dinefwr, looking towards the remains of the late thirteenth-century middle gate passage. The raised area to the right may have formed the outer ward proper and possibly housed service buildings. The lower ground to the left perhaps accommodated the medieval residential settlement.

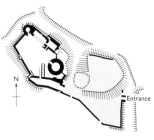

Part of the deep rock-cut ditch, the outer line of defence, which cut off the end of the long, rocky ridge on which the castle was built.

The Outer Ward

On approaching the castle (near the first information panel on the left), notice the deep rock-cut ditch on either side of the track. This is the outer line of defence, which served to cut off the end of this long, rocky ridge, protected naturally by steep slopes on all other sides. The track passes over the ditch, but there must originally have been a bridge here and probably a gate, of which little remains save for some low footings on either side. Fragments of the defensive stone wall, which would have surrounded the outer ward, survive and can be seen from the track above the ditch to the left.

The bailey, or outer ward, into which you now pass, has two levels. The ground is lower to the left, with a higher level to your right. These levels are part natural and part created by terracing, producing two flattish areas on the sloping ground. It is possible that they served different functions. The upper level, for example, may have formed the outer ward proper, whereas the lower may have formed part of the earliest attendant residential settlement, which later developed into a small town (p. 27).

The two-ward layout of the castle as a whole may well be a feature that goes back to the earliest phase of construction. On such a narrow cliff as this, options for castle design were limited. Nothing now survives save some areas of levelling to suggest what buildings once stood in this outer ward. We do know from documents that two large and three small buildings were erected in the bailey in 1282, though we are not given any clue as to their function. Service buildings, such as brewhouses, stabling and barns, were often housed in the outer bailey of the medieval castle.

Today, the outer ward is part of the SSSI, managed as a summer meadow, and is the home of flora of particular importance. In May, the bailey is particularly beautiful, when it abounds with bluebells.

Ahead, the track passes quite close to the rock cliff on the left, and, almost for the first time, you can appreciate the natural defensive qualities on this southern side of the site. The sheer drop, well nigh impregnable from attack, also affords extensive views down the flat land of the Tywi valley. On a clear day, the castle of Dryslwyn can be seen standing on its isolated hillock to the right of the early nineteenth-century Paxton's Tower. Despite its position on the cliff edge, this side of the castle is defended by a stone wall, now somewhat reduced in height, which runs from the outer ditch to join the masonry of the inner ward.

The Towns around the Castles

In thirteenth-century Deheubarth, as elsewhere in native Wales, the demands and needs of the royal court would have provided the context for the growth of nucleated settlements. It might be too sweeping to describe all of these as towns, though 'proto-urban' communities certainly appear to have nestled under the walls of the castles at both Dinefwr and Dryslwyn.

In the wake of the Edwardian conquest, a new town was established at each site and the surviving documentation tells us much more of the development of urbanization. At Dinefwr, in 1280, King Edward's surveyors noted the *villa de Scleygon* (the vill of the clerks), which may refer to the residences of the administrators who would have needed to be near to the Welsh prince's seat, and which may have been the precursor of the later town. In 1281, Edward granted the town the right to hold a weekly market and an annual fair as part of his policy to encourage urban development, as well as strengthening the supply base for foodstuffs for his garrisons. By 1298 the fledgling borough contained twenty-six burgages, with a mill, reeve (administrator), and a court.

A few years later, in 1303, a clear distinction was made in the expanding settlement between the 'new' (or 'lower') town to the north and the 'old' (or 'upper') town on the castle hill. The thirteen burgages in the old town were all let to Welsh tenants at a reduced rent of 6d. per year, whereas the thirty-five tenants in the new town (many of whom were immigrants) were paying the normal rent of 1s. a year. A survey made in 1360 reveals the vitality of both the towns at Dinefwr, with as many as forty-six burgages available in 'Y Drenewydd', the new town.

In 1392, King Richard II (1377–99) granted the burgesses of Dinefwr equal legal status to those of Carmarthen and their continuing prosperity seemed assured. Thereafter, however, the towns seem to have made little progress and they suffered from the ravages of plague, and from the military action during the Owain Glyn Dŵr revolt (p. 19). Subsequently, the general lack of interest by the Crown and its agents in maintaining these outlying properties gave free rein to the rapacious tendencies of local noblemen, turning once flourishing towns into sections of their estates. By the early fifteenth century there was little to distinguish the old and new towns, though Y Drenewydd continued to elect a mayor as late as 1651. The new town, described as 'nowe ruinus' by John Leland in the 1530s, seems to have been swept away by the building of Newton House. Both towns were evidently overshadowed by the more suitably positioned town of Llandeilo, probably indeed older than either, and which, of course, has continued to be a prominent Welsh market town to the present day.

The history of the town at Dryslwyn is similar. In 1281, it too was granted a charter by Edward I to hold a fair for four days starting on St Bartholomew's Day, so the town was almost certainly in existence by then. In 1294, it was expanded with a grant of thirty-seven new burgages, apparently let to immigrant settlers who were English, Gascon or Flemish in origin. There was a grant of a weekly market in 1324, and by the 1350s there were thirty-four burgage plots in the town and fourteen outside the town on 'Budge Street' or 'Briggestrete'. It seems, however, that the Black Death took a terrible toll at Dryslwyn, and the destruction of the castle deprived the town of the income derived from the wages of the garrison. Consequently, economy and population declined until by the seventeenth century the town was virtually abandoned.

The towns of Dinefwr and Dryslwyn were granted the right to hold a weekly market in 1281 and 1324 respectively. This early fourteenth-century manuscript illustration shows traders at a market stall selling bread (The Bodleian Library, Ms. Bodley 264, f. 204r).

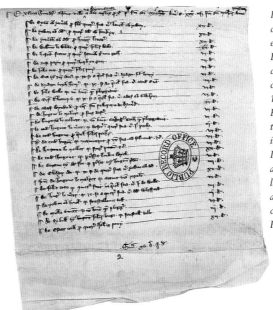

In the wake of the Edwardian conquest new towns were established at both Dinefwr and Dryslwyn. The only surviving court roll from the hundred court at Dinefwr, dating from 1302–03, records Welsh and English, women and men, and tradespeople and traders locked in combat at law and in the town. It paints a picture of the social and administrative realities of life in the two towns at Dinefwr at the beginning of the fourteenth century (The National Archives: PRO, SC 2/215/17 f. 2).

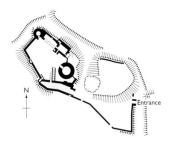

Above: The footings of the second Welsh gate, built sometime before the 1270s. The steps presumably led to the wall-walk around the gate.

Below left: Dinefwr's gate-passage, built after 1277, would have served to channel people towards a new gate into the inner ward.

Below right: The arrowloops, chamfered door jambs and drawbar hole are almost all that remain of the inner gate ordered in 1282–83, most probably by Robert Tibetot, the English justiciar of west Wales.

The Middle and Inner Gates

At the far end of the outer ward, the track approaches the inner line of defence, comprising a rock-cut ditch and gate. Notice how the ditch immediately to the right has been considerably enlarged by modern quarrying, perhaps by estate workers needing stone for castle repairs. Also visible is the massive bulk of the great circular keep standing on the highest point of the site, a rock outcrop which rises directly from the base of the ditch. The rock is friable here and a large section of the curtain wall has collapsed leaving it uncertain whether it originally surrounded the keep completely, or if (as at Dryslwyn) it joined the keep allowing its circular wall to form part of the inner ward defences.

Continue on across the ditch — where there would once have been a bridge — into what is, in effect, a gate-passage. Within the slight remains of the masonry here, there are fragments of three different phases of gate. Originally, the gate here would have been a simple opening through the curtain wall, which would have run straight to the rock face. In the second phase, this early Welsh gate was strengthened, probably before the 1270s, with the addition of a gatehouse running internally from the curtain. You can see the slight footings of its surviving northern side at ground level on the right, further in towards the castle. Steps at the side presumably led to the wall-walk around the gate. In the third phase, probably dating to the English occupation from the years after 1277, the gate was strengthened once again, this time with the addition

of more massive masonry, which projected out over the earlier ditch. This is the more impressive stonework on your right, though once again too little survives to show any details.

Entry into the passage must have been restricted by a door and portcullis, in a similar fashion to the better-preserved and near-contemporary gate at Dryslwyn (pp. 45–46). Here at Dinefwr, the new Edwardian gate necessitated recutting the defensive ditch further out, and this may be the digging exercise that is referred to in the documentation of the 1280s (p. 10).

As completed, the late thirteenth-century gate-passage was quite long, and also rather unusual. Notice the high battlemented wall on the left, which in fact clings perilously close to the cliff edge. But the passage is dominated by the curtain wall on the right, built in part on what had been the Welsh gate, during the English modifications to the castle sometime after 1277. The narrow gate-passage served to channel people toward a brand-new gate into the inner ward.

At the entrance, with its modern wooden door, the details of the Edwardian inner gate are visible. The arch and right-hand jamb of the original opening can be seen clearly, though the whole has been partially blocked to produce a more manageable doorway. Notice, too, the small blocked window above and to the left.

Walking in through the gate, on your right you will see two plain arrowloops and beyond them a deep drawbar hole that housed a beam used to secure the gate. On either side, though hidden, we know there are decorated stops at the bases of the chamfered

The Inner Ward

door jambs. Of red sandstone, these stops are of a late thirteenth-century type, and seem to confirm that this was indeed the gate ordered in 1282–83 by Robert Tibetot, the English justiciar of west Wales, at a cost of £12 13s. 4d. The stops, arrowloops, drawbar hole, arched opening, and the blocked window adjacent are all that now remain of the gatehouse. The west side of the structure, that to the left of the passage, was almost entirely removed, whereas that to the east was drastically converted to the present stair in the seventeenth century to give access to the new summerhouse. In all, it is very difficult to be sure of the appearance of this late thirteenth-century gatehouse.

The compact, almost intimate, nature of the inner ward courtyard is striking. The angularity of the shape, its high defensive wall with five changes of angle over relatively short distances, and the height and bulk of the towers produce an almost claustrophobic effect. In the medieval period this would have been even more overwhelming, since the inner wall of the hall has now fallen, and — as windows and rooflines testify — there must have been several other buildings against the surrounding walls.

The compact inner ward at Dinefwr, looking east towards its much-altered keep and with the northern chamber block on the left.

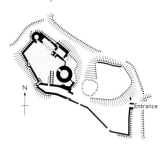

Opposite: Standing on a rocky outcrop, the Welsh-built keep still dominates the entire castle. It now consists of a single floor above a basement, topped by the seventeenth-century summerhouse, but the original tower could have risen to two floors. In this view from the exterior, the gently sloping — battered — walls and stringcourse of creamy Bath Stone are clearly visible. From this point you also get the best view of both broken ends of the curtain wall and can imagine their junction at either the north-east corner or at the keep itself.

This view into the keep at Dinefwr, from wall-walk level, shows one of the ground-floor-level windows with its steeply raking sill (bottom). Above, there is the faint outline of a blocked window with window seats. The square-headed windows and cupboards at the top belong to the seventeenth-century summerhouse.

The Keep

To the right of the inner gate, the huge round tower immediately demands our attention. It is better preserved than its neighbour at Dryslwyn, though both these Deheubarth keeps were undoubtedly similar in origin. Here, notice the ground-floor entrance, a later insertion, but for the moment let us consider the exterior details.

To begin with, the tower was probably entered by way of an external stair to a doorway at first-floor level, now blocked (though visible from inside). The tower stands on a rock outcrop, the floor of its basement laid directly upon the natural rock surface. The massive battered walls at the base of the tower are topped with a roll moulding, a stringcourse of creamy Bath Stone, which must have been imported to the site. Above, the walls are vertical and featureless save for three small windows set at an equal distance one from another; only one is visible from this point. All have been altered from their original shape, beginning as long narrow slits, constructed more for ventilation than for light. With their steeply raking internal sills, the windows were meant to serve the otherwise unlit basement.

Several other circular towers of this type — found widely across the southern March — are thought to date from the 1230s. Generally, those found at Anglo-Norman castles have two storeys set over a ground-floor basement. Here, at Dinefwr, the basement and first floor survive intact, but any upper floor that originally stood here, along with the wall-walk and parapet, has been taken down and replaced by a summerhouse. You can see how the much thinner walls of this 'pleasance' more or less perch on top of the massive thirteenth-century tower. In turn, the summerhouse walls are punctuated with large rectangular windows and a door. A number of drawings show that it had a conical roof when it was built in the late seventeenth century, which evidently became a conspicuous feature of the landscape (pp. 21–23).

Now go into the tower through the ground-floor entrance, a modification that perhaps dates to the fourteenth century and which involved a breach through the massive base of the lower walls. On the left of the door is a long curving hole in the masonry. This is probably the remains of timber bracing for the initial structure, which was disturbed and cut through when the doorway was inserted. Inside, the floor of the basement was originally of flagstones; the position

of the ceiling is indicated by joist holes and an offset within the walls. Ventilated and lit by the three slit windows already referred to, and accessible by trap door or internal ladder from above, the basement was probably used for storage.

Look up to your right, where — in an area of surface lime concretion — you can see the faint outline of the thirteenth-century doorway into the tower. Externally, it is blocked by the post-medieval stair. Directly opposite, there is the outline of a window, with seats, which is also blocked. Above this, where there may have been an upper medieval floor, the masonry now represents the late seventeenth-century summerhouse, broken by square-headed windows, a fireplace, cupboards and a door. The summerhouse rises directly from the inner wall face of the keep. Indeed, such is the smoothness of the masonry that there seems little doubt that the internal wall face of the keep was substantially refaced by the Dynevor Estate, at which time the lower slit-window embrasures may also have been remodelled.

The Inner Ward Wall-Walk

On leaving the keep, climb the broad stair alongside it. Built to enable visitors to promenade on the wall-walks in the seventeenth-century, the stair was considerably rebuilt during repairs to the castle in the nineteenth century. On reaching the wall-walk, turn left and go back towards the keep.

Passing over the arched 'bridge' into the summerhouse, remember that the thirteenth-century door into the keep is directly below you. As you walk around the outside of the summerhouse, notice how thin the walls are compared with the thickness of the thirteenth-century masonry underfoot. Though the summerhouse itself is ruined, and is bereft of roof and floor, you can of course share much the same glorious views over the estate parkland and the Tywi valley enjoyed by those eighteenth-century travellers before you.

Return to the stair, but continue around the wall-walk towards the west. This route soon passes over a small rectangular turret, which marks the change of wall direction adjacent to the inner gate. Just beyond, an inconspicuous latrine chute was probably added in the fourteenth century. From this position you can easily appreciate the precipitous edge of the rock cliff on which this side of the castle perches, and which made the site so significant as a point of defence.

The inner ward wall-walk now provides extensive views of the beautiful Tywi valley with Dryslwyn Castle in the distance. From here, however, you can also appreciate the defensive strength of the site as the curtain wall rises almost directly from the precipitous cliff below.

Right: Seen in detail, the lower levels of the north-west tower indicate the scale of modifications and rebuilding that took place during the Edwardian alterations to the castle.

Continue along the crenellated wall-walk to the south-west corner, noting the absence of any tower at this position. Originally, the wall-walk passed through the north-west tower, behind the hall and northern chamber block, and continued around the north-east corner of the castle to return to the keep. However, the whole of the north-east section of the inner ward curtain wall has fallen, probably due to the collapse of the friable bedrock on which it stood. A thin modern blocking wall now fills the gap between the chamber block and the keep. Continue along the western wall-walk to the north-west tower.

The North-West Tower

From the wall top, you can see that this small circular tower was built against the existing defensive wall to overlook and control the ridge of high land to the west. Raised as part of the Welsh castle, as additional defence opposite the keep, it must have been a grim, cramped and comfortless place, built entirely for military purposes.

Enter the tower and turn left up the mural stair to the small landing in front of the doorway to the upper floor. From here you have a good view of the internal wall-walk at roof level, which was accessed via a small lookout turret. You can see how the wall-walk would have continued through the doorway opposite onto the north curtain wall (now inaccessible). The top of the tower is crowned by estate-period crenellations.

There are two internal floors, neither of which enjoys the comfort of a fireplace. The upper floor has a window overlooking the north-western approaches and access to the wall-walks on the south-west and north-east curtains. A mural stair led to the small lookout turret on the north-east. This echoes the similar turret on the chamber block and may well be an Edwardian or later addition. It is clear that the tower functioned primarily to service military requirements, with a wide field of vision at high level, and provided shelter and intercommunicating access to wall-walks.

Climb down the steep internal steps to the ground floor of the tower. The lower floor, set over an apparently solid base, is higher than the courtyard and is now entered through an opening that was originally the only window at this level. A mural passage through an adjacent doorway leads now to a latrine shared with the hall, contrived in the space between the tower and the wall of the hall range. It was this door which probably served as the original entrance to the tower, with steps up from the courtyard against the curtain wall. The rough third doorway — through which you have just passed —together with its steps was inserted for the convenience of visitors during the Picturesque period and does not conform to any medieval floor level. Access between the two floors may initially have been via a mural stair, blocked during the Edwardian alterations.

The results of the geophysical survey of the two Roman forts overlaid on an aerial photograph of Dinefwr Park. The characteristic playing-card shape of the two superimposed forts is clearly visible (National Trust/Stratascan).

The Roman Forts in Dinefwr Park

A Roman fort had long been suspected near Llandeilo. As well as reports of spasmodic discoveries of Roman material during the nineteenth century, including fragments from a possible mosaic, there was a tantalizing gap between the forts at Llandovery and Carmarthen. Yet it was not until 2003 that geophysical survey confirmed the presence of not one but two Roman forts, on high ground in the north-east corner of Dinefwr Park, near the drive to Newton House. Little remains visible above ground, as the land has been ploughed for some considerable time, but initial excavations have suggested more information about the date and layout of the military site. We now believe that a fort was first established here in the AD 70s, during the initial Roman incursions into south-west Wales. At 9.1 acres (3.84ha), it is one of the largest forts in Wales and must have housed a substantial military detachment — at least a cavalry squad (*ala quingenaria*) or a large infantry or mixed unit (*cohors milliaria*). It was, however, short lived, abandoned perhaps due to the necessity of moving troops to campaigns in northern Britain and elsewhere in the period AD 78–83.

It may have been the subsequent disengagement of troops from Scotland that allowed the return of Roman forces to Llandeilo and the re-establishment of a fort on the same site late in the first century AD. This smaller fort (3.8 acres, 1.54 ha), overlying the north-east corner of its larger predecessor, may have held a small infantry unit (*cohors quingenaria peditiata*) and appears to have been occupied for a much longer period of time.

Excavations have shown that both forts had timber and earthen defences, with timber buildings inside. The road leading north-east from the front entrance of the fort has been traced and a *vicus* or civilian settlement grew up outside the military confines, providing evidence of the interaction between native people, camp followers and the Roman soldiers. Characteristically, the later fort was abandoned in the early second century, conforming to a pattern of apparent demilitarization of south-west Wales at this time and it seems that the *vicus* may have then spread to within the former military defences. The spectacular geophysical plan of the forts shows that they lie relatively intact within the parkland, offering scope for further work to assist our understanding of Roman Wales.

The excavation of the forts has produced pottery dating to between AD 70 and AD 140 suggesting that they were established during the reign of the Emperor Vespasian (AD 69–79) and that the garrison at Llandeilo was withdrawn early in the second century AD. This urn, shown as revealed by excavators, remains remarkably intact (Cambria Archaeology).

The kitchen was possibly situated against the curtain wall to the south of the north-west tower, conveniently located to serve the hall. This illustration, from the fourteenth-century Luttrell Psalter, *shows a cook and servant preparing food for diners in the hall (British Library, Additional Ms. 42130, f. 207v).*

Several features suggest that the tower was originally circular in form, and that the courtyard face was later rebuilt flat when the lookout turret was added. Perhaps these were the repairs to the 'little tower' referred to in the building accounts of 1282–83 (p. 10). Later still, the wall-walk was brought around in front of the tower, probably when a range of buildings was added to the south and the hall block raised to the east. This created the existing, rather inconvenient, stepped entrance, with the tower hemmed in by the new buildings to either side. Interestingly, given that the entrance was now equipped with a drawbar hole in the added masonry on the outside, the tower may have served by this date as a strongroom or prison.

Just south of the tower, a rectangular window in the curtain wall is all that survives of the building that must originally have stood in this position. The curtain has been substantially refaced during the estate-period repairs, and there is no evidence to indicate the length or height of the building, never mind suggest its function. It is tempting to think that it may have been the kitchen range as it is conveniently situated to provide for the adjacent hall, but not so near as to offer a fire risk. The remaining stretches of curtain wall are featureless below the wall-walk.

From here, return to the base of the steps to the keep.

The Northern Chamber Block

The rectangular block directly in front of you was built to provide comfortable accommodation (see reconstruction drawing). Finely dressed stone, incorporating a number of the red sandstone jambs and stops of the type already noted in the detail of the inner gatehouse, was used throughout the building. In its present form, the chamber block is largely a late thirteenth- to early fourteenth-century structure, which projects beyond the line of the earlier Welsh curtain wall. With two well-appointed upper floors over a partial basement, these were clearly the best rooms in the castle at this time and may have been occupied by the constable and his family, or high-ranking guests.

A cutaway reconstruction of the Edwardian northern chamber block and later hall at Dinefwr to suggest their internal arrangements during the Hakeluts' custody of the castle during the first quarter of the fourteenth century (Illustration by Chris Jones-Jenkins, 1999).

Notice the clear structural joint, which runs vertically in the wall face of the main block [**A**]. This suggests that the whole building was extended eastwards; there are, however, reasons for supposing that within the masonry of this building there are remnants of a smaller and much altered pre-Edwardian structure, built against the Welsh curtain wall. This was perhaps the hall used by the Deheubarth princes. If so, it may have been of similar dimensions to the original great hall at Dryslwyn. This, too, was built against part of the inner ward curtain wall, though it was to be much altered, probably in the 1280s (pp. 12–13).

Also Welsh in origin, but obscured by the modern wall to the right (south-east) of the chamber block, there was a two-storey wing with a room on each floor. Adjoining the chamber block and built against the original Welsh curtain wall, this wing has now fallen and the details of its relationship to the main block are difficult to disentangle.

Before entering the chamber block, notice the small blocked window on the first floor [**B**]. It seems likely that all the courtyard windows were originally of this form. They were later enlarged, perhaps with the general refurbishment undertaken in the first half of the fourteenth century.

The porch, which covers the main entry to the block, was created when the external stair to the first floor was remodelled, probably in the eighteenth century. Note how the chamfered door jambs, with their decorative stops, demonstrate not only the quality of the medieval building, but also indicate a floor level considerably higher than that of the later porch with its bench seats. It seems that the late thirteenth-century ground level inside and immediately outside the building has been lowered. This is also a good place to note several characteristic repairs carried out by the Dynevor Estate. On the right-hand side of the door, for example, the original jamb stones give way to plain dressed-stone blocks; and the lintel has been replaced by iron bars that pass behind the porch masonry.

Once inside, it is possible to appreciate the medieval arrangements, despite the partial collapse of the outer wall and estate repairs to the west wall, which has been substantially refaced. The basement was reached by way of a steep flight of external steps from the courtyard and entered by a well-built doorway with a low and massive lintel. Featureless save for its two ventilation slits, the basement now only extends part of the way across the block.

In its present form, the northern chamber block at Dinefwr is largely a late thirteenth- to early fourteenth-century structure, perhaps built over the remains of the Welsh hall used by the Deheubarth princes.

The height of the chamfered door jambs, with their decorative stops, demonstrate that the medieval floor level must have been much higher.

Although there is now no indication of its function, the limited light and lack of heat suggest that the basement was used for storage.

Above, the wooden floor of the ground-floor room (once supported by massive joists) has fallen; so too has the wooden ceiling, which was supported by very fine corbels. This chamber was well lit by two large windows overlooking the sloping ground to the north. Both had seats to enable the occupants to take full advantage of the light and pleasant views. A third window looked out into the courtyard. The chamber was heated by a fireplace between the two northern windows, though only part of its base survives, together with a few remaining stones of the chimney flue above. The small doorway in the north-west corner leads to a well-preserved latrine in a turret lit by two small windows rebated to take wooden shutters. Even the bolt holes for the shutters are still visible. Another doorway — with jambs and decorative stops similar to those already noted — once led to the projecting wing at the south-eastern end of the range. This doorway was blocked by the estate after the wing itself had collapsed. A third internal doorway at this level led into the ground floor of the rectangular hall block.

Access to the apartments on the first floor was gained by way of an external flight of steps, situated in much the same position as the ruinous estate-period staircase. In the main commodious upper chamber there were three windows overlooking the courtyard. As noted from outside, it was perhaps in the fourteenth century that two of these were much altered and enlarged. The third window was blocked and converted into a cupboard, though its original form with its window seats remains clear. As first built, all three openings were probably of this smaller form. Additional windows gave views outside the curtain and the fireplace may have been located in a similar position to that in the room below. Doorways also occupy the same positions as those on the lower floor. That leading to the former south-eastern wing is now partially shut off and the doorway in the west wall, which connected to the hall, is totally blocked. The third door gave access to another well-appointed latrine in the turret at the north-west angle of the block and thence to a lookout position high above.

A modern stair now leads from the ground floor to these upper levels. At the top, you can progress through to the latrine turret and, from here, climb the stair to the wall-walk level, noting the finely dressed stonework on your way. Through the grille in the floor of the wall-walk, it is possible to see the original doorway that linked the upper chamber to the hall, now blocked up on both sides. The turret stair, meanwhile, continues to the lookout position at the very top, where there are fine views in all directions.

When you return to ground level, leave the chamber block and turn right to look at the hall range.

The Hall

The hall would have been at the centre of life at the castle throughout its history. Here, the castle community would have gathered for both social and formal occasions, official meetings and the dispensation of justice. And yet, it is clear from the building evidence (see pp. 10–11, 38) that the remains of the hall that we see today must have been built after the adjacent chamber block, no doubt replacing an earlier hall elsewhere in the castle. Like its neighbour, the hall protruded beyond the line of the original Welsh curtain wall, and similar detailing

The interior of the northern chamber block. This suite consisted of two well-appointed chambers, served by a private latrine turret, and contains some of the finest carved stone in the castle.

between the two buildings suggests that they are not far apart in date.

The wall on the courtyard side of the hall range has fallen, though its position is clear from the broken stump of masonry on the south-western angle. The hall itself was situated on the first floor, and was presumably approached by way of an external stair. A large window and adjacent fireplace survive in the north wall, and the door in the north-west corner led to a latrine. Another door provided direct access to the upper room in the chamber block. The ground floor may have been used for storage and would have been accessed separately.

Notice how the west wall of the hall is squeezed up against the north-west corner tower. In fact, this new work blocked the original entrance to the tower, which itself lay against the curtain wall. The building of the hall range and chamber block necessitated the demolition of much of the original northern line of the inner ward curtain wall and entirely changed the external form of this corner of the castle (pp. 10–11).

The Southern Curtain and Turret

There is no tower at the south-west corner of the inner ward and the wall turns abruptly to follow the sheer drop of the rock ledge along the southern side. Though the wall has been entirely refaced internally, during estate-period repairs, a ground-level arch visible on the exterior suggests that there may have been a sally port, or postern doorway, in this corner. Just to the east of this, there is a small latrine contrived largely within the thickness of the wall, though with a slight external projection. Nearby, notice the short length of solid masonry on the line of the inner parapet (parados) wall, perhaps indicating the former presence of a gable of another courtyard building.

The rectangular turret at the change of angle on the southern curtain effectively overlooks the entrance passage. It was probably added to the castle after the Edwardian conquest as part of the new defences and housed one small chamber with a latrine set over a solid basement built around double latrine chutes. During the Picturesque period, it was substantially altered to provide a second, albeit subtler, summerhouse.

The new hall, built in the early fourteenth century, substantially altered the arrangements of the north-west corner of the inner ward. Its position between the chamber block and north-west tower is marked by the fireplace in the curtain wall.

The short length of solid masonry on the inner southern curtain wall may indicate the former presence of another courtyard building.

The first-floor room is entered by a door from an external stone stair. Inside, the wall plaster and tiled floor date from the summerhouse period, as do the two large windows; the southern one was probably converted from an original, while that to the west was inserted to provide outstanding views over the river. A medieval window on the east — helpful for defence in that it overlooked the entrance passage, but providing no panoramic views — was blocked in the later period when timber housing was installed to support either panelling or decoration. A modern grille inserted in the tile floor shows the chutes below.

This tower is kept locked to protect the delicate decorative plasterwork inside, but access for pre-booked tours can be provided on application to Cadw.

The rectangular turret at the change of angle on the southern curtain wall. The latrine chutes are medieval; the upper levels, however, were remodelled into a summerhouse during the Picturesque period.

The Exterior of the Castle

Before leaving Dinefwr, it is well worth walking around the castle to view its defences from the outside. Retrace your steps along the entrance passage, but turn left outside the middle gate. Here, the curtain turns abruptly to run north, but, after only a very short stretch, it is broken off, having collapsed where the friable rock must have given way. The broken wall was later faced by estate workers to prevent further collapse, and a thin piece of modern walling was built to block the gap between the curtain and keep. The keep wall itself has been underpinned in modern times to prevent it from sliding down the slope. You can see, far above you, the continuation of the stringcourse around the keep and, just above this, one of the three small basement slits.

Turning the north-east corner, the ditch profile — widened by quarrying — returns to the normal medieval width, though there is evidence here of landscaping work in the Picturesque period. Above, there are the remains of the small building adjacent to the chamber block, invisible from within because of the modern infill wall (p. 35). The two blocked doors in its rendered west wall are clearly visible. But the curtain, which formed its northern wall, has fallen; so too have the east and most of the south walls. From this point you get the best view of both broken ends of the curtain wall and can imagine their original course to their junction either at the north-east corner or at the round keep.

Further along the ditch on the north side it is possible to appreciate the massive build of the chamber block with its fine quoins, battered base and north-west latrine turret. Butted on to this is the hall range, again with fine dressed quoins on the north-west corner. Its wall-walk is carried on high corbels as it turns towards the north-west tower and it is clear that the earlier curtain was demolished in order to provide a suitable rectangular area for the new building. This extraordinary alteration completely compromised the defensive strength of the earlier circular tower at the north-west angle of the castle.

The very different build of the north-west tower reinforces the suggestion that it is of Welsh construction. Seen from outside, it is largely featureless save for one window at the upper-floor level and the estate-period crenellations on the top.

But its height, standing guard over this corner of the ditch, is impressive. The curtain on the west is clearly earlier than the tower; the plain masonry is only relieved by a single window and by the crenellations along the wall-walk.

Walk around the west ditch to the south-west corner and climb the steps to the lookout point, behind which you can see the surviving sides and springers of the blocked sally port door. Note the projecting masonry of the mural latrine just in front of you, and, further along, high on the wall masonry, the corbels of the discharge from a small open latrine on the wall-walk. The large Picturesque-period west window of the south turret can be seen, below which are the medieval double latrine chutes, which indicate the original function of this small projecting tower. Retrace your steps along the western ditch to the north-west corner.

The Welsh Town

One contender for the position of the town at Dinefwr is now just below you. A flattish oval area, apparently terraced into the hillside and bounded on the north by an earthen bank may be the original site of the town, or it is perhaps the 'castle garden' referred to in documentation. As previously noted, the woods along the ridge to the east of the castle are naturally terraced and perhaps the town expanded eastward to encircle the castle on two sides. We can but speculate on the forms of the houses and the size of the plots occupied by the burgesses, or townspeople, of the town nestling at the foot of the castle.

From here you can return to the car park at Newton House using the waymarked footpaths.

Continuing along the northern exterior of Dinefwr, the remains of the two-storey wing adjacent to the chamber block are clearly visible. Particularly impressive, however, is the massive build of the chamber block with its fine quoins, battered base, and north-west latrine turret.

This 1779 aquatint of Dinefwr by Paul Sandby (d. 1809) exemplifies the ideal of the Picturesque. The jagged ruin of the castle contrasts with the managed landscaped park and its cattle, deer, and aristocratic figure on horseback (National Library of Wales).

Dinefwr Park

Emma Plunkett-Dillon

Dinefwr Castle was rescued from crumbling decay by the ambitions of the Rice family, descendants of Sir Rhys ap Thomas and occupiers of Newton House. From the middle of the seventeenth century onwards, successive generations appreciated the significance of the castle both as a viewpoint from which to admire Dinefwr Park and as a Romantic ruin silhouetted against the southern sky.

In the 1750s George Rice, and his wife Cecil, absorbed the newly fashionable concept that gardens should reflect the perspective of the landscape painter and that formality, straight lines and right angles should be abandoned in favour of a naturalistic interpretation. They set about creating what was to become one of the finest parks in Britain. Accounts record acquisition of lands, clearance of hedges and removal of buildings, but only to the east of Newton House. Fortunately for them Dinefwr had several essential components already in place; stands of mature trees within the deer park, flowing water, interesting topography and, overlooking it all, the battlements and towers of the castle. Unlike many of his contemporaries, George Rice did not have to invest in the requisite artificial ruin and to compound this advantage his castle reflected centuries of honourable history. After his visit in 1775 Capability Brown commented: 'I wish my journey may prove of use to the place, which if it should, it will be very flattering to me. Nature has been truly bountiful and art has done no harm'.

As the century progressed, tastes moved to the Picturesque — a wilder, more rugged attitude to landscape design. One of the leading advocates of this approach, William Gilpin, was inspired greatly by what he saw at Dinefwr, citing the splendid trees and 'great variety of ground'. No doubt he was referring to the wooded rocky knolls that characterize the western and southern part of the park. The Rice family therefore found themselves praised for a landscape they had done little to enhance. It could be described as opportune that a fire, sometime prior to 1787, which partly destroyed the summerhouse, enhanced the Picturesque nature of the castle. Numerous artists and writers visited recording their impressions in journals, sketches, paintings, poems and even on a dinner plate, part of a service commissioned by Catherine the Great of Russia (d. 1796). Richard Fenton admiring the park in 1807 from Llandeilo Bridge described it as 'a charming view of the loveliest spot my eyes ever beheld'.

The park remains relatively unaltered to this day. From the castle towers one can still appreciate the achievements of George and Cecil Rice. Two types of spatial composition converge at Newton House. To the west and south-west open spaces are enclosed with continuous woodland and rugged knolls with tightly framed views. In contrast, to the east, wide vistas encompass rolling landforms with planting confined to regimented clumps, some of which encase remnants of earlier formal avenues. Some intermingling occurs with fingers of woodland extending the Picturesque elements towards Llandeilo. Sinuous drives and circular paths present spectacular views towards the house and castle, and the river valley beyond.

The National Trust is working with its partners Cadw and the Wildlife Trust of South and West Wales to restore and enhance the eighteenth-century design. Modern fencing has been removed, paths and drives restored, vistas reinstated and new trees planted. Improved biodiversity will not only benefit wildlife but will also restore the texture and colour of the grass swards. Interpretation in Newton House explains the key elements of the park, encouraging visitors to explore and enjoy this remarkable and utterly beautiful landscape.

Looking north-east from the castle, the late eighteenth-century planting scheme of regimented clumps of trees is clearly visible.

Below: Newton House and the surrounding parkland of the Dinefwr Estate viewed from the north-west (© NTPL/ Andrew Butler).

A Tour of Dryslwyn Castle

Dryslwyn stands prominently atop a small and steep-sided hill at the centre of the broad Tywi valley. Barely 4 miles (6.4km) south-west of Dinefwr, and directly overlooking the river, for much of the Middle Ages the castle controlled one of the few crossing points on this meandering stretch of water above Carmarthen. In the shadow of the castle ruins, across the northern stretch of the hillside, are the earthwork remains of Dryslwyn's attendant medieval borough. Initially, the river itself was crossed by way of a ford, but by the 1350s there was a bridge — when as many as fourteen of the borough house plots were set out on 'Briggestrete'. This most likely was the latest in a succession of medieval and later bridges.

The Medieval Town and its Defences

The suggested route of this tour begins at the car park below the western side of the hill. Having crossed the main road, you will find a gateway leading to modern steps and a gravel path. As you ascend the fairly steep climb to the castle, it becomes much easier to appreciate the true defensive nature of the site.

Just after a further group of modern steps, where the path takes a right-handed turn, you will be standing directly outside the western gatehouse into what had become, by the fourteenth century, a well-established

Opposite: A view from the banks of the Tywi river to the dramatically sited remains of Dryslwyn Castle.

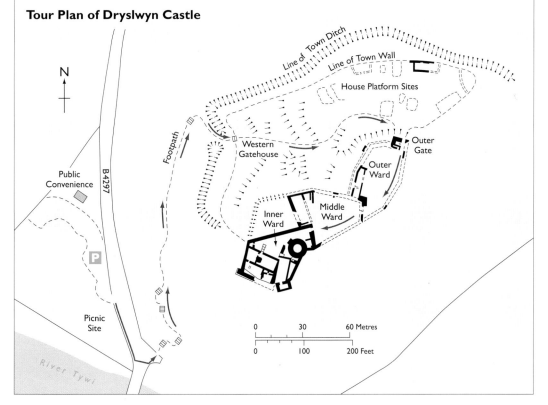

Tour Plan of Dryslwyn Castle

N

Line of Town Ditch
Line of Town Wall
House Platform Sites
Footpath
Western Gatehouse
Outer Gate
Outer Ward
Public Convenience
B 4297
Middle Ward
Inner Ward
P
Picnic Site

0   30   60 Metres
0   100   200 Feet

River Tywi

The castle is on top of a steep hill. From the car park cross the road and go through a kissing gate onto a steep gravel path with steps. The castle area is rough grass with some stone steps.

Well-defended gatehouse entrances were a feature of the new towns raised by Edward I. The twin-towered Upper Gate at Conwy is a good example; the gatehouse at Dryslwyn, however, is likely to have been smaller and less elaborate.

town or borough (p. 27). A narrow road or trackway, formed on a flattened bedrock surface, ran up to this gate throughout the later Middle Ages.

To either side of the gate, above an already steeply raking bank, the town walls probably stood up to 7 feet (2.1m) high. Today, at the base of what remains a significant slope, to the left in particular you will see a shallow trench — all that remains of the original town ditch. Cut into bedrock, this defensive ditch was over 16 feet (5m) wide and 8 feet (2.5m) deep. Here, immediately in front of the gate, the ditch was spanned by a wooden bridge, which led to the entrance passage.

A small Welsh town, surrounded with a rock-cut ditch, probably existed on this hill before the Edwardian siege of 1287, since in his account of expenses for the following two years Alan de Plucknet recorded the work of diggers 'repairing the fosses (ditches) round the vill (town)'. The borough was expanded and the town walls and western gateway were added in the late thirteenth century, possibly by Rhys ap Maredudd in the 1280s or in the years following the English capture of the castle in 1287. Indeed, well-defended gatehouse entrances were a feature of the new towns raised by King Edward I and his barons in the wake of the late thirteenth-century Welsh wars. Other examples, somewhat larger than Dryslwyn, include the gates that survive at Caernarfon, Conwy and Denbigh.

As completed, the Dryslwyn town gate was probably of two storeys with a small guard-chamber over the entrance passage. Very few traces of masonry

survive above ground, though close to the edges of the path you will see the slots in which a portcullis was raised and lowered from above. Behind the slots there are simple rebates for the wooden gate.

Beyond the west gatehouse, the footpath is less formal, though you should follow the line of wooden marker posts, climbing through the heart of the medieval town of Dryslwyn. On either side of the path are traces of rather crudely flattened terraces cut into the sloping hillside. These are the deliberately created platforms representing the burgage plots on which the houses of the town once stood. In the first half of the fourteenth century, there were at least thirty-four houses within the defences, as well as granaries and other buildings for animals and storage.

If the evidence of an excavated example of these houses is typical, they were fairly small rectangular structures, approximately 35 feet (10.7m) long by 15 feet (4.6m) wide. The rough stone walls, no more than a few courses high, were probably intended to support a wooden frame containing wattle panels covered with clay daub, presumably limewashed to make the whole waterproof. The floors inside medieval houses such as these were often of beaten clay, though with frequent use they could be worn through to bedrock. Roofs were probably made of thatch or wooden shingles since no traces of slate or stone tiles were recovered in excavation. It is also worth noting that nineteenth-century farm buildings constructed using much the same framing technique can still be seen in the Tywi valley.

An aerial view of Dryslwyn from the north-west. Traces of a flattened terrace cut into the hillside survive below the steep scarp slope in the foreground to the left of this picture. This represents a burgage plot on which one of the houses of the medieval town once stood.

The Castle Gatehouse and the Outer Ward

Near the last of the wooden marker posts, as the path levels out, you must turn to the right to explore the remains of the castle. First, however, take a moment to appreciate the overall plan (see inside back cover). In the far distance, above the river, the prominent stonework belongs to the inner ward, initially raised in the early thirteenth century. The middle and outer wards, which extend towards you along the ridge, were added in later phases of Welsh occupation. Here, at what represents the easternmost limit of the late thirteenth-century fortifications, the visitor enters the outer ward alongside the castle's main (outer) gatehouse.

In what is now a hollow-way below the remains of the gatehouse, the main road, which led to both the medieval town and castle, can be followed north-eastwards along the side of the hill. Overlooked by both a stretch of the town walls and the outer

gatehouse, the route was clearly well defended. Should you wish to, it is well worth walking partway down this road to view another section of the town ditch, and from there to appreciate further aspects of the defensive nature of the site.

The largely overgrown remains of the outer gatehouse itself are situated beneath and to the side of the large ash tree. As completed, this two-storey structure was approached from the town by way of a wooden bridge or drawbridge spanning what was then a defensive ditch. In fact, the main approach road to the town ran along the base of this same ditch (see reconstruction, p. 18), now represented by the hollow-way. Apart from the ruinous nature of the remains — with much of the eastern half of the gatehouse fallen away — interpretation of the original arrangements is further complicated by the fact that the entrance passage was blocked with rubble walling, probably when the castle was abandoned in the early fifteenth century.

Nevertheless, traces of portcullis slots survive at either end of the blocked gatehouse passage and a stone rebate behind the rear slot indicates

A view from the outer gatehouse looking along the ridge towards the inner ward, the heart of the medieval castle. The strongly defended outer ward was probably built by Rhys ap Maredudd late in the thirteenth century. Not only did it provide additional protection but also extra accommodation for stables and other ancillary buildings.

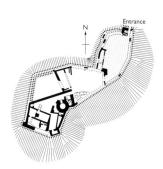

the position of a wooden door. Therefore, the gate as a whole was probably defended by a paired sequence of portcullis and doors near the outer and inner ends of the passage. A similar arrangement can be seen in many late thirteenth- and fourteenth-century gatehouses across Wales and further afield. Would-be entrants might be admitted past the initial portcullis and gates to be questioned in the passage. If all was well, they were permitted to pass through the second set of gates and portcullis into the castle itself.

The ruinous remains of Dryslwyn's outer gatehouse viewed from the south. As completed, this two-storey structure was approached from the town by way of a wooden bridge or drawbridge spanning what was then a defensive ditch.

A stone-vaulted passage, in which the remains of steps survive, ran up from the back of the gatehouse and gave access to the chamber over the passage. It was here that guards would have operated the winches that raised and lowered the two portcullises.

With your back to the gatehouse, you must imagine a substantial stone wall running along both sides of the outer ward. It was slightly less than 6 feet (1.8m) thick, and stood on top of an earth bank. A small section survives to a height of almost 10 feet (3m). On the west side (the right as you continue walking), a revetment wall was added to the base of the bank immediately after the siege of 1287. It was constructed in squared stonework, especially characteristic of this period. Excavation has revealed that the walls here and elsewhere in the castle were originally covered in limewash, doubtless making it a very prominent feature on the valley skyline.

You must imagine, too, an interior filled with buildings such as stables and stores, together with halls or houses providing accommodation for soldiers and officials. Traces of the stone walls of at least one large building

During excavation of the great hall, fragments of a fine window with cinquefoil cusps, carved from red sandstone, were discovered in the north wall of the range (Illustration, Chris Jones-Jenkins, after Caple, 1996).

Dryslwyn: Archaeology and Castle Life

The finds retrieved from the archaeological excavations at Dryslwyn have shown us that those who lived here, particularly the Welsh lords Maredudd ap Rhys and Rhys ap Maredudd, led a far more comfortable life than the now bare stone walls might suggest. The castle was well built, and its walls covered in a mortar coating. Limewash was regularly applied to the exterior and many interior walls. Some of the internal chambers were decorated with painted plaster. The lords looked out of finely carved stone windows, and a few fragments of glass suggest that even by the mid-thirteenth century — when most windows were open or simply had wooden shutters — Dryslwyn contained some glazed windows.

The lords of Dryslwyn and their followers wore clothes decorated with ornate jewellery brooches and rings. They ate fine foods, as indicated by the bones of cattle, sheep, pig, deer, and many different game birds (such as partridge, woodcock, snipe, and

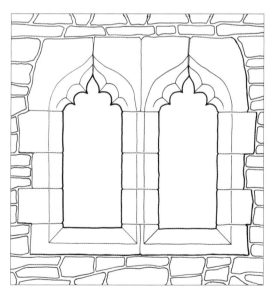

mallard), as well as various types of fish (including salmon, trout, pike, cod, plaice, herring, mackerel, haddock and hake). Much of this was doubtless eaten with root vegetables, which leave no archaeological trace. The recovery of grains of oats and rye, together with a quern stone for grinding flour, can be seen in the south-west or right-hand corner of the ward, though its specific function is unknown. Almost all of the castle's internal buildings — in all three wards — were built in the same fashion, their walls butting against the inner face of the surrounding defences.

The Middle Ward

As you pass through the southern end of the outer ward, traces of a thick, angled wall protecting the northern corner of the middle ward are visible. Nearby there was a gateway linking the two enclosures. No trace of a gatehouse was found in the archaeological excavations and it appears that there must have been a simple gate through the wall. Nevertheless, when it was first built in the mid-thirteenth century, this was the main castle gate. In fact, there may have been a tower alongside the gateway, behind the protective angled wall. It could be the fallen masonry from this demolished tower that forms the small hillock you have passed on your right.

At the far right-hand end of the middle ward, the walls of a large hall running north to south were uncovered during excavation. Now grass covered, the hall was built up against the western defences of the ward itself. Traces of a cellar were also revealed to the east. In the rather narrow space, between what was the southern gable end of the hall and the external face of the inner ward, there was a narrow passageway. From here, garrison soldiers could climb the steps to the wall-walk around the middle ward curtain wall.

At right angles to the face of the northern curtain wall, two parallel low walls mark the early and late phases of another stone-built hall or house. This structure ran for some distance to the east of these walls. The excavations revealed that there were several phases in both the wall and floor construction of this building. The domestic nature of occupation in this and other buildings of the middle ward is attested by the many fragments of imported French pottery — Saintonge ware — recovered from the rubbish deposits beneath the floors.

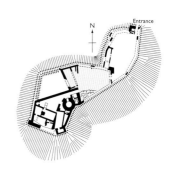

suggests that bread or flatcakes were also consumed. Fruits were eaten: seeds of raspberries, cherries and blackberries have been recovered. More surprising were the finds of grape and fig seeds, probably dried fruits imported from Gascony in south-west France. Such fine cuisine was very little different from that which is recorded as being consumed by the household of King Edward I.

Within the many layers of stone and earth excavated at the site, other archaeological finds included bone, pottery, arrowheads, nails, and (though rare) the occasional coin. All of these help us to date the various layers, and tell us something of what people were doing at the time the layers were deposited. In all, many thousands of finds were recovered.

During the excavations of the north-west corner of the midden area (p. 55), the removal of a layer of building rubble revealed the base of a latrine pit, which still preserved its medieval contents. The rotted material included patches of a white lime, doubtless thrown into the latrine during use to act as an antiseptic and to reduce the smell. Excavation of the material revealed that it only survived to a depth of 4 inches (10cm). The upper levels of the pit

or shaft had been dug away in later periods. At the very bottom of the pit, a corroded bronze horse spur was discovered. Analysis of samples of the soil from the latrine revealed a variety of small seeds and fish bones, which had been digested by the castle's inhabitants. The discovery of parasitic worms and the pupae of flies confirmed the interpretation of the remains as coming from a medieval latrine.

Amongst the finds excavated at Dryslwyn are this remarkable bronze macehead (above), discovered in the mid-thirteenth-century layers of a cesspit beneath the courtyard, and (left) a selection of spindle whorls, gaming pieces, a carved bone pin head in the shape of a dragon, a knife, a quill pen nib, and a little copper-alloy brooch (Chris Caple).

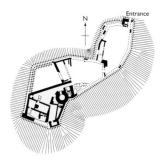

The Inner Ward

The south-west end of the ridge was occupied by the inner ward, always the heart of a medieval castle. As noted, it was initially raised in the second quarter of the thirteenth century, but was completely remodelled at the time of Rhys ap Maredudd, probably during the 1280s. Further minor modifications were made after the English occupation of Dryslwyn in 1287, right through to the mid-fourteenth century. Traces of all the principal phases survive above ground. Moreover, the whole area has been excavated, revealing a great deal, not only about the various details of construction, but also about the people who lived here.

The large rock outcrop to the left of the entrance into the inner ward was originally of even greater size. After the great Edwardian siege, workers were employed 'breaking a rock at the entrance to the castle'. The outcrop was thus deliberately reduced to facilitate modified entrance arrangements.

The Gateway

This said, the form of the inner ward gateway is essentially that created in the 1280s by Rhys ap Maredudd. More advanced than the earlier middle ward gateway, it comprised two quite separate gates at the inner and outer ends of a short, open passage. In turn, such improved defensive arrangements were to be superseded by the planning introduced to the massive gatehouses built at Edward I's castles in

north Wales. At Dryslwyn, we see some of this growing sophistication in the late thirteenth-century outer ward gatehouse (pp. 45–46).

In the outer part of this particular gateway, there are slots for a portcullis sitting in front of rebates for a two-leaf wooden door. Grooves or holes in the walls behind the rebates were found to contain lead. It provided the seating into which the iron hinges of the gates were once set. The gates and even the iron hinges, like many of the castle's other valuable features, were removed during a period of looting after the site was abandoned, but before it was demolished.

Inside what is effectively an outer gate, there is a ramped passage leading to an inner gateway. Here, too, there is evidence for the original door hinges, as well as a deep hole in the left-hand wall behind the position of the gate. The wooden drawbar, which sat in this hole, would have been drawn across to secure the gates when they were closed.

Beside the sloping passageway, there is a small wall which creates a modest platform. On this platform, the archaeological excavations recovered the charred remains of a guardhouse which had been burnt to the ground. Originally, it was a timber-framed building, probably with wattle-and-daub panelling, of similar construction to the houses in the town. Its roof, however, was of slate rather than thatch. From here, during the late fourteenth-century phase, guards would have controlled access through into the inner ward.

Beside the guardhouse, there is a flight of steps leading up to a landing, and from here another set of steps climbed to the wall-walk. Traces of an arch springing out from near the top of the higher flight of steps suggests that there was direct access from the wall-walk to the adjacent round tower. The wall-walk itself went all the way around the top of the gate area, and the winch controlling the outer portcullis must have been operated from this level.

Apart from the small timber-framed guardhouse, the central area between the inner and outer gates may have been open to the weather. One other feature to note at this point is the blocked opening in the wall which stood between the back of the guardhouse and the landing. This may well indicate that there was an earlier enclosed stone guard-chamber in the gatehouse area, lit in part by this window. On the other hand, castle defenders on the

Dryslwyn Castle underwent various phases of rebuilding and modification throughout its history. Stonemasons, as shown in this early fourteenth-century manuscript illustration, would have been amongst the labourers employed to undertake this work (British Library, Cotton Nero Ms. D I, f. 23v).

The sloping passage of Dryslwyn's inner ward gateway, which controlled access between the middle and inner wards. Closed by gates at either end of the passage, the entrance was also defended by a portcullis.

landing may have used the opening to enquire of, or even fire at, would-be entrants in the central gate area. The opening was certainly blocked when the timber guardhouse was built.

It is also important to appreciate that the line of the inner gate marks the approximate position of the entrance to the original Welsh castle. Invariably, examples of main gates into most thirteenth-century native castles tend to be rather small — sufficient perhaps for no more than people on foot or for a pony. They were usually located in a section of the main castle wall, immediately beside a major tower, as at Llywelyn ap Gruffudd's stronghold at Dolforwyn in Powys, as well as at Dinefwr. Here, at Dryslwyn, the Welsh gate was reached by way of steps that were recovered during the excavations. The modifications made during the remodelling of the inner ward in the 1280s were clearly intended to strengthen the defences at this point. They would also have allowed for wider access, perhaps by wheeled vehicles. In all, as it survives, this Dryslwyn gate is a rare example of a composite dual entrance.

The Courtyard

Having passed through the gate complex, you enter the inner ward courtyard. On your immediate left is the base of the great round tower, and to the right is the inner ward curtain wall. Today, the curtain has a curved appearance as a result of a huge piece of the round tower falling on it during the demolition of the castle.

As noted elsewhere, the castle appears to have been decommissioned in the earlier fifteenth century. Later it was looted, with those building materials of any value removed. Subsequent burning added to the process of destruction and, finally, the buildings of the inner ward appear to have been very deliberately pulled down. As a consequence, the rubble which was removed during the excavations — many tons of it — was fresh and unweathered. Moreover, the archaeological remains of the castle's occupation lay undisturbed beneath the destruction debris.

In the early thirteenth century, the surface on the eastern side of the courtyard was a simple platform

The inner ward gateway. Archaeological excavations revealed evidence of a guardhouse on the small grassed platform overlooking the gate-passage.

The keep at Dryslwyn does not survive to its full height, but it may have stood to two storeys above the basement. Like the round tower at Dinefwr, it was originally entered at first-floor level; the ground-floor entrance is a later insertion.

Dolbadarn Castle has the finest surviving example of a Welsh round tower. Built by Llywelyn ab Iorwerth in the early to mid-thirteenth century, it was probably modelled on English examples in the southern March.

of flattened bedrock with a levelling of dumped earth and stone, whereas the western side was formed over the natural hillside. Some areas were used for penning animals, whilst others were occupied by middens of dumped rubbish. Later, a latrine pit was dug into the surface near the northern curtain wall. In this pit, a bronze macehead was recovered, together with fragments of pottery (p. 47). Later, the courtyard was filled with earth and stone and covered with a mortar surface; a large set of steps down to the cellar of the great hall was also added. The mortar surface was repaired many times over the decades of occupation.

The Round Tower (The Welsh Keep)

A narrow passage through the thickness of the wall led into what was originally the basement of the great round tower. The walls at this point are more than 10 feet (3m) thick. As noted at Dinefwr (p. 30), similar towers with characteristically flared bases are found in both native and Anglo-Norman castles across much of Wales. The Anglo-Norman examples usually feature two storeys above the basement. This

may have been the case here and at Dinefwr although, elsewhere, Welsh towers — of whatever shape — tend to have one upper level only. Generally built in the early to mid-thirteenth century to serve as keeps, other examples include Pembroke in the south-west, Bronllys and Skenfrith in the south-east, together with Dolbadarn and the somewhat later Dolforwyn in the north.

Almost invariably, in their original form, all of these towers were entered at first-floor level. Although here at Dryslwyn the tower does not survive to this height, the presence of an external buttress, replaced at least three times during the life of the castle, suggests that the original first-floor entrance was on the north-western side. The stair was probably made of wood and supported by the stone buttress.

Initially, access into the basement of the tower would have been by way of an internal ladder down from the first floor. The ground surface was covered with fine flagstones, though this presumably dark chamber was perhaps used for no more than the storage of supplies or perhaps as a prison. Fragments of the flagstones, which were broken and removed at a later date, can still be seen at the base of the inner walls. The ground-floor passage was created from a hole knocked into the lower walls late in the tower's history. As at Dinefwr, this modification probably belongs to the English period of occupation, when the notion of defending such a keep in isolation was no longer necessary. The passage would have made entry into the basement from the rest of the castle easier. It almost certainly continued in use for storage, with the door to the passage opening from the courtyard side. A wall was built to block the passage when the castle was decommissioned.

Prison

In the western corner of the courtyard, there is a small building in the angle between the curtain wall and the great hall. A doorway in the outer wall would have contained a door that opened outwards. Inside, the original floor was sunk down below the courtyard level. Given the door arrangement, this building is perhaps best interpreted as the castle prison. If so, this is where the lords of Dryslwyn at some time incarcerated felons, hostages and adversaries — even kinfolk.

The Great Hall

Running from east to west across the southern half of the inner ward courtyard is the great hall, referred to in the fourteenth century as the 'King's Hall' (pp. 12–13). A broad flight of steps leads down into what was the basement level or cellar.

Although the overall structural history of the building is a little complex, most aspects can be understood by looking carefully at the upstanding detail, and by reference to the information recovered during the excavations. To begin with, in the mid-thirteenth century, the hall itself occupied a single upper storey over the basement. The stone plinth, which survives near the middle of the basement, rose to support a central hearth or fireplace within the hall. A section of the chimney, recovered during the excavations, can be seen beside the stone plinth. At this same time, the level of the wooden floor within the hall was somewhat higher than the present offsets in the side walls. In fact, it would have been closer to that of the courtyard. Originally, the now-blocked arrowloop in the southern face of the building (better observed from outside) would have helped to light the basement, and the hall floor must have been situated above this.

The great hall would have been at the centre of castle life and used for social and formal occasions, official meetings and the dispensation of justice. This fourteenth-century manuscript illustration shows a lord dining with his wife and guests; a cup-bearer kneels before him (British Library, Additional Ms. 42130, f. 208).

The stone plinth, which survives near the middle of the basement of Dryslwyn's great hall range, once rose to support a central hearth in the first-floor hall above. A section of the chimney, recovered during excavation, now rests on a concrete platform beside the plinth.

A cutaway reconstruction of the great hall range at Dryslwyn, showing the internal arrangements as they may have appeared after Rhys ap Maredudd's substantial remodelling of this area of the castle during the 1280s (Illustration by Chris Jones-Jenkins, 1999).

Archaeological excavations uncovered much of the evidence for the later form of the great hall range at Dryslwyn Castle (David Robinson).

When the inner ward was remodelled in the 1280s, the building was transformed — at least across much of its eastern half — so as to include two upper storeys over the basement. And it was during these changes that the wooden floor immediately above the basement was lowered. As noted, you can see the offsets which supported the wooden beams running along the north and south walls. In the east wall, the large socket and stone corbel supported another wooden floor beam running at right-angles. In turn, the central stone plinth was altered to provide a seating for this beam. Taken as a whole, the evidence suggests that the first-floor level was probably lowered to create room for the insertion of another storey above this same end of the building.

Meanwhile, beyond a cross-wall, the single upper storey arrangement may well have been retained in the western half of the building. Notice the window in the basement level of the north wall, which is almost certainly a modified arrowloop belonging to the original hall. There are slight differences in build between the two sides of this window.

Below the window, and running across the ground surface, there is a stone-capped drain. It can be traced back to the foot of the basement steps, and was designed to remove water coming down from the courtyard. The drain prevented the water spilling into the cellar itself. This was particularly important since, as an early fourteenth-century document records, 'the cellar under the hall [was] where all the garniture and victuals were stored'.

Further evidence for the later form of the entire great hall range was recovered from the excavations. It was covered with a substantial slate roof, which crashed into the basement during the fifteenth-century fire. A few glazed ceramic floor tiles were also found, and these are likely to have formed the floor around the first-floor hearth. In the north wall of the range, there was a fine window with cinquefoil cusps, carved from red sandstone (p. 46). Also recovered from the burnt deposits were several iron hinges for the wooden doors of the building. The largest of these was over 3 feet (0.9m) in length.

South Side Apartment Block

On leaving the western end of the great hall range, via the later phase steps in the southern wall, you enter an area which — in the early thirteenth century — served as an open courtyard. In the south-west corner, overlooking the river, you will see the low foundations of a good stretch of original inner ward curtain wall. The ground level within the contemporary castle was well below the present surface.

In the late thirteenth century, a new building containing rooms or apartments on two floors was built across the entire courtyard area, running parallel to the south side of the great hall range. The huge wall, which now dominates the southern side of the castle, was the outer wall of this block of apartments. The floor level throughout the area was raised to a point just below the windows in the massive southern wall. In turn, this floor level ran across to match that in the first storey of the modified great hall range.

The rooms within the apartment block were on two levels, corresponding with the two storeys seen in the hall range. All were fitted with large windows looking out over the Tywi. Indeed, the grandeur of this rebuilding of the south side of the castle was clearly designed to impress those who saw it. From the archaeological and architectural evidence, it seems unlikely that these apartments (as well as the corresponding changes in the great hall range) were

raised before the third quarter of the thirteenth century. And, it is difficult to accept that such elaborate reconstruction would have taken place after 1287; nor is there any record of such expenditure. It seems likely, therefore, that the redevelopment of the inner ward was the work of Rhys ap Maredudd, probably in the early to mid-1280s. Both the apartments and the hall would have been occupied by Rhys and his family, together with their important guests. Then, following the siege and capture of Dryslwyn in 1287, the accommodation would have been used by the English constables serving the Crown.

Seen from this same southern area, it is noticeable that the outer face of the western end of the great hall range is rather poorly finished. This probably reflects the remedial work of 1338–39, when 'the western side of the King's Hall' was said to be 'entirely decayed through old age and fallen to the ground'. This must have occurred after the raising of the floor level and the construction of the apartment block. The façade of the rebuilt wall would not have been seen, and so did not need to be properly faced.

The small cross-wall, which separated the two halves of the apartment block, was a later addition; it contained a doorway at first-floor level. Beyond this cross-wall, a large section of the massive southern wall of the block is missing. It was deliberately brought down during the fifteenth-century demolition of the stronghold.

A view across the courtyard at Dryslwyn, towards the substantial remains of the southern apartment block. Paxton's Tower (above) a Picturesque folly constructed during the early nineteenth century, is clearly visible in the distance to the south-west (© NTPL/Chris Warren).

Throughout the castle's history the kitchen was located to the south of the great hall, originally free-standing but later incorporated within the walls of the apartment block. This fourteenth-century manuscript illustration shows a servant cooking food in a cauldron over a log fire, a scene that was no doubt mirrored in the kitchen at Dryslwyn (British Library, Additional Ms. 42130, f. 207).

You will also notice the low walls of an early stone building in this area. As built, this structure would have stood in the initial open courtyard, and was fitted with a doorway and steps leading towards the great hall. With a large hearth at the centre, it seems likely that this would have served as the kitchen, built separately from other buildings so as to avoid the risk of fire. The steps would have provided access from the kitchen to the higher early level at which the floor in the great hall range was set.

The eastern part of the kitchen was obliterated by the construction of the end wall of the apartment block. Meanwhile, with the ground level raised, the demolished debris of the remainder of this early kitchen was buried. A large drainage trough — set into the floor — was uncovered by excavation in the north-east corner of the apartment block. This suggests that, although rebuilt, this area continued to serve as a kitchen during the later phases of the castle's occupation.

The Great Chamber and the Chapel

Following the path within the modern railing, the route out of the apartment block area takes you into a quite large rectangular structure running down the slope from north to south, now known as the great chamber.

The earliest archaeological phases excavated in this part of the castle tell us that initially there was a sequence of wooden buildings. These abutted the great hall range, and the later examples had substantial

In the fourteenth century, the Benedictine nuns of St Mary's Priory in Chester were required to provide a chaplain to hold services in the castle chapel at Dryslwyn three times a week. This near-contemporary manuscript illustration shows a priest raising the Host during Mass, watched by members of the Butler family of Wem, Shropshire, in their private chapel (The Walters Art Museum, Baltimore, Ms. W 105, f. 15).

clay floors. To the south, within the early thirteenth-century curtain wall, there is evidence of a small postern gate. It was reached by a series of crude steps cut into the clay bank. Outside the postern there was a platform which provided access down further steps to the hillside. At the base of the hill, at roughly this point, lay the original ford by which travellers crossed the Tywi. The postern was guarded by a simple door, and is probably identical in form to the main entrance into the early thirteenth-century castle.

In the mid-thirteenth century, when Maredudd ap Rhys was lord of Dryslwyn, the stone structure which is now visible replaced the earlier wooden buildings. At the northern end of what began as a single-storey block, the bases of two narrow windows are just visible. These may well have been glazed. The great chamber had a fine mortar floor with wooden internal partitions. At the southern end, it appears that the great chamber would have backed on to the initial curtain wall. However, this would have meant that the postern gate was situated below ground level, and it is by no means clear how it was approached, or even if it was still in use in this period.

Towards the end of the thirteenth century, probably during the extensive work of the 1280s, a new large tower was built out over the river, beyond the original castle wall, and supported on the earlier platform. This fairly massive construction contains three lancet windows in its outer face, and appears to have been the castle chapel. As such, the chapel was situated at the same level as the upper floor of the adjoining block of apartments. Almost certainly, it would have served Rhys ap Maredudd as the last Welsh lord of Dryslwyn, as well as the subsequent constables of the castle and their households. In the fourteenth century, it is known that the Benedictine nuns of St Mary's Priory in Chester — who were responsible for the local parish church at Llangathen — were required to provide a chaplain to hold services in the castle chapel at Dryslwyn three times a week. Thus the chapel clearly continued in use into the later phases of occupation at the site.

Substantial changes were made to the great chamber during the 1280s. The north windows were partially or completely blocked and a wooden floor was inserted, creating a first-floor chamber over a basement. As modified, this chamber was probably at the same level as the chapel and the upper apartments in the adjacent blocks. The wooden floor was replaced during the fourteenth century.

Access Platform

Leaving the great chamber at the northern end, you arrive back in the main courtyard. From here, around to the right, you will find a flight of steps climbing to an external platform. Throughout the history of the castle, this platform served to give access to different areas. In the initial Welsh castle, it probably led, via wooden steps, to the stone buttress outside the round tower (p. 50), and from there to the first-floor entrance into the tower itself.

In the 1280s, when the great chamber was converted to a two-storey structure, new steps up from the courtyard and a mortar surface were added to the platform. A plinth or platform was also built against the north wall of the great chamber to provide access to its upper storey. Wear patterns on the mortar floor provided a strong indication of numerous people having climbed the stair up on to the platform and into the upper level of the hall.

Midden Area

Squeezed in behind the great chamber and the inner ward curtain wall, there is a triangular-shaped area. Before the construction of the great chamber, this space was occupied by the wooden buildings with clay floors mentioned above. But with the great chamber in place, it became something of a redundant area.

Initially, a good deal of building rubble was dumped into the area, and it was discovered that a

The great chamber complex occupied the grassed area in the foreground of this view. Beyond, the three lancet windows indicate the position of the castle chapel.

Two stone latrines were built into the thickness of the late thirteenth-century east curtain wall. This view shows the chutes, through which the waste was channelled, emerging on the outer face of the wall.

latrine had been dug into this. In subsequent years it was used as the castle midden, with the waste from the castle kitchen being dumped over the surface. Evidence from parasites preserved in the excavated soil suggests that pigs were also kept in the area. Next, the eastern wall, from the southern end of this midden area to the round tower, was rebuilt. This probably followed the demolition of the original castle wall during the siege of 1287. Note the use of squared limestone blocks in this later rebuilding, compared to the random masonry used in the construction of earlier Welsh buildings such as the great chamber. On completion of the new eastern wall, the midden passed out of use and was capped with a surface of mortar and slate.

Access to the Latrine

As part of the reconstruction of the eastern wall, a large and steep flight of steps was built to provide access to the wall-walk. Fragments of the wall-walk, which ran all round the inner ward, can still be seen at the top of the southern apartment block.

Between this new flight of steps and the round tower, a small corridor was created and given a mortar floor. This corridor led to a set of spiral steps, which in turn gave access to a pair of stone latrines built in the thickness of the replacement east wall. Originally, the latrines were totally enclosed within a passage in the wall. They had wooden seating and a superstructure perched above stone chutes discharging the waste outside the castle walls.

Further Reading

Acknowledgements
The authors and Cadw would like to acknowledge Professor J. Beverley Smith, Professor R. A. Griffiths and the late Professor Sir Rees Davies for their help with this guidebook.

R. Allen Brown, H. M. Colvin and A. J. Taylor, *The History of the King's Works, II, The Middle Ages* (London 1963), pp. 641–44.

Chris Caple, 'The Castle and Lifestyle of a 13th Century Independent Welsh Lord: Excavations at Dryslwyn Castle 1980–1988', *Château Gaillard* **14** (1990), 47–59.

R. R. Davies, *Conquest, Coexistence, and Change: Wales 1063–1415* (Oxford 1987); reprinted in paperback as, *The Age of Conquest: Wales 1063–1415* (Oxford 1991).

Ralph A. Griffiths, *The Principality of Wales in the Later Middle Ages: The Structure and Personnel of Government, I, South Wales, 1277–1536* (Cardiff 1972).

Ralph A. Griffiths, 'The Revolt of Rhys ap Maredudd, 1287–8', *Welsh History Review* **3** (1966–67), 121–43; reprinted in Ralph A. Griffiths, *Conquerors and Conquered in Medieval Wales* (Stroud 1994), pp. 67–83.

Ralph A. Griffiths, 'A Tale of Two Towns: Llandeilo Fawr and Dinefwr in the Middle Ages', in Heather James, editor, *Sir Gâr: Studies in Carmarthenshire History* (Carmarthen 1991), pp. 205–26.

Ralph A. Griffiths, *Sir Rhys ap Thomas and his Family* (Cardiff 1993).

E. A. Lewis, 'Dynevor: Materials Illustrating the History of Dynevor and Newton from the Earliest Times to the Close of the Reign of Henry VIII', *West Wales Historical Records*, 1 (1910–11), 145–224.

J. E. Lloyd, editor, *A History of Carmarthenshire*, 2 volumes (Cardiff 1935–39).

Donald Moore, 'Dynevor Castle and Newton House: Some Seventeenth-Century Pictures', *Archaeologia Cambrensis* **143** (1994), 204–35.

J. E. Morris, *The Welsh Wars of Edward I* (Oxford 1901); reprinted (Stroud 1997).

M. Prestwich, *Edward I* (London 1988); new edition (New Haven and London 1997).

Sian Rees, *A Guide to Ancient and Historic Wales: Dyfed* (London 1992).

D. F. Renn, 'The Round Keeps of the Brecon Region', *Archaeologia Cambrensis* **110** (1961), 129–43.

Myvanwy Rhys, editor, *Ministers' Accounts for West Wales, 1277–1306*, Cymmrodorion Record Series, 13, (London 1936).

J. Beverley Smith, 'The "Cronica de Wallia" and the Dynasty of Dinefwr', *Bulletin of the Board of Celtic Studies* **20** (1962–64), 261–82.

J. Beverley Smith, 'The Origins of the Revolt of Rhys ap Maredudd', *Bulletin of the Board of Celtic Studies* **21** (1964–66), 151–163.

J. Beverley Smith, 'Treftadaeth Deheubarth', in Nerys Ann Jones and Huw Pryce, editors, *Yr Arglwydd Rhys* (Cardiff 1996), pp. 18–52.

J. Beverley Smith, *Llywelyn ap Gruffudd, Prince of Wales* (Cardiff 1998).

Anne Solomon, *The Last Siege of Dryslwyn Castle* (Carmarthen 1982).

Roger Turvey, 'The Defences of Twelfth-Century Deheubarth and the Castle Strategy of the Lord Rhys', *Archaeologia Cambrensis* **144** (1995), 103–32.

Roger Turvey, *The Lord Rhys: Prince of Deheubarth* (Llandysul 1997).

Roger Turvey, *The Welsh Princes 1066–1282* (London 2002)

Peter Webster, 'Dryslwyn Castle', in J. R. Kenyon and R. Avent, editors, *Castles in Wales and the Marches* (Cardiff 1987), pp. 89–104.